ARBITRATION AND STATE ENTERPRISES

ARBITRATION AND STATE ENTERPRISES

A survey on the national and international state of law and practice

by

KARL-HEINZ BÖCKSTIEGEL

Prof. Dr. jur.
Chair of International Business Law
Cologne University

AN INTERNATIONAL RESEARCH STUDY OF THE
Institute of International Business Law and Practice
OF THE
International Chamber of Commerce

KLUWER LAW AND TAXATION PUBLISHERS
Deventer/Boston

Kluwer Law and Taxation Publishers
P.O. Box 23
7400 GA Deventer
The Netherlands

Tel.: 31-5700-47261
Telex: 49295
Fax: 31-5700-22244

Library of Congress Cataloging in Publication Data

Böckstiegel, Karl Heinz.
Arbitration and state enterprises.

'In international research of the Institute of International Business Law and Practice of the International Chamber of Commerce.'
Bibliography: p.
1. Arbitration and award. 2. Government business enterprises—Law and legislation. I. Institute of International Business Law and Practice. II. Title.
K2400.B63 1984 346'.07'0269 84–14408
ISBN 90–6544–184–0 342.670269

First published in 1984

ISBN 90 6544 184 0

TABLE OF CONTENTS

CHAPTER I

THE INSTITUTE OF INTERNATIONAL BUSINESS LAW AND PRACTICE

The rapid growth of international trade and the development of the mechanisms by which it is regulated led the ICC, in 1979, to call upon academics and practitioners active in the field of international trade to set up a non-profit organization for research and training, the Institute of International Business Law and Practice.

GOALS

Made up of lawyers and practitioners from all over the world and functioning in complete scientific independence, the Institute has set itself these goals:

- to encourage the study of legal points relating to international trade;
- to foster a wider knowledge of international trade law;
- to strengthen the links between academics and practitioners;
- to provide lawyers, businessmen, researchers and students with means to deepen their knowledge of the legal techniques of international trade and to enable them to apply those techniques in practice.

STRUCTURE

THE ACADEMIC COUNCIL

The overall orientation of the Institute is determined by an Academic Council of 40 members appointed by the President of the ICC upon the suggestion of the Council. Members are chosen among persons throughout the world who are known for their skill and activity in the field of international business law.

THE EXECUTIVE COMMITTEE

This Committee is a smaller body which is responsible for deciding how the Council's recommendations are to be put into effect.

Corresponding Members

The Academic Council names corresponding members who are responsible for sponsoring the Institute's work on a regional basis. They are chosen from the business world, from universities and from international organizations. Their task is to support the Institute's work and make it known in their respective countries and to ensure the necessary liaison with the representatives of their own professions.

Subscribing Members

The corporate bodies who wish to support financially the activities of the Institute can be appointed subscribing members. These members will benefit from a preferential tariff of fees at meetings and from the distribution of documents of limited circulation.

ACTIVITIES

Seminars, Colloquia, Conferences

The Institute's programme of work includes the organization of seminars on international contracts and on international commercial arbitration. The seminars include contract negotiation and simulated arbitration based on real cases. The Institute also holds colloquia and conferences on current themes in international business law. These meetings are held either at ICC Headquarters or abroad, at the invitation of ICC National Committees and other bodies.

Examples of Themes at Recent Institute Conferences

- Performance Bonds and Contract Guarantees.
- The International Effects of Nationalisation.
- The Role of Engineers in Preparing, Drafting and Executing International Contracts.
- The Mechanisms of International Trade.

Research

In addition to its training activities, the Institute both initiates and supports research projects entrusted to recognized specialists in the field of international trade. The most advanced projects are:

(a) Arbitration and State Enterprises

The purpose of this study is to analyse and define as accurately as possible the conduct of State-controlled enterprises in relation to international commercial arbitration. A detailed survey was carried out in different countries among the arbitral institutions, lawyers and academics. The conclusions are of topical importance, particularly as a growing number of public bodies participate today in international trade relations.

(b) Interpretation and Application of International Trade Usages

This study has already made it possible to analyse a number of legal and arbitral decisions which involve the question of the recognition of international trade usages and practices. The answers vary from one country to another and it may be desirable to launch a standardization drive either within the ICC or with other international bodies.

(c) Cost Reimbursement Contracts

When it comes to major construction and development projects, the work involved is of such large scale that it is often difficult to arrive at an overall estimate of the costs of completing the project. In such a case, the parties can choose to adopt the cost reimbursement system, rather than a classic lump-sum contract. This study aims to provide potential users of such contracts with background information and recommendations that can help them in negotiating and executing the contracts.

PUBLICATIONS

- *Multiparty Business Disputes*: publication No. 359.
- *Interpretation and Application of International Trade Usages*: publication No. 374.
- *Performance Bonds and Contract Guarantees*: published jointly with the International Bar Association.

MEMBERS OF THE ACADEMIC COUNCIL*

CHAIRMAN OF THE INSTITUTE

*Pierre Lalive***
Professor at the University of Geneva and at the 'Institut des Hautes Etudes Internationales'

SECRETARY GENERAL OF THE INTERNATIONAL CHAMBER OF COMMERCE

*Hans Koenig***

MEMBERS OF THE ACADEMIC COUNCIL

Bola Adesumbo AJIBOLA,** Legal Practitioner, Lagos.
Pierre BELLET, First Honorary President, Cour de Cassation, Paris.
Giorgio BERNINI, Professor, University of Bologna.
Karl-Heinz BÖCKSTIEGEL, Chair of International Business Law, University of Cologne.
Pasquale CHIOMENTI, Chairman of the ICC Commission on International Commercial Practice, Lausanne.
William Laurence CRAIG, Attorney-at-law, Coudert Brothers, Paris.
Bernado CREMADES, Attorney-at-law, Madrid.
J. Michael EDWARDS, Q.C., Provost, City of London Polytechnic.
Florentino P. FELICIANO,** Attorney-at-Law, Sycip, Salazar, Feliciano e Hernandez, Manila.
Marcel FONTAINE, Professor, Université Catholique de Louvain.
Michel GAUDET,** Chairman of the Court of Arbitration of the ICC, Paris.
Ottoarndt GLOSSNER,** Chairman of the ICC Commission on International Arbitration; Attorney-at-Law, Kronberg.
Berthold GOLDMAN, Professeur émérite de l'Université de droit, d'économie et de sciences sociales de Paris.
Lars HJERNER, Professor, University of Stockholm.
Eduardo JIMENEZ DE ARECHAGA, Attorney-at-law, Montevideo; Former President of the International Court of Justice.
Djamal LAKHDARI, Attorney-at-law, Paris.
Mark LITTMAN, Q.C., Barrister, London.
Bruno OPPETIT,** Professor, Université de droit, d'économie et de sciences sociales, Paris; Director of the research at the Institute.
Tudor POPESCU, Professor, University of Bucharest.
Jan RAMBERG, Professor, University of Stockholm.
Pieter SANDERS, Professor, University of Rotterdam.
Ignaz SEIDL-HOHENVELDERN, Professor, University of Vienna.

* This list is regularly amended. For further information, please contact the Secretariat of the Institute, 38 Cours Albert 1er – 75008 Paris.
** Members of the Executive Committee.

John R. STEVENSON, Attorney-at-law, Sullivan & Cromwell, New York.
Rolf STOEDTER,** Chairman of the International Maritime Arbitration Organization, Hamburg.
Arthur VON MEHREN, Professor, Harvard Law School, Cambridge.

CORRESPONDING MEMBERS*

A. SCHOLARS

Mr. Ayo AJOMO
Department of Jurisprudence and International Law
University of Lagos
Lagos, Nigeria

Prof. Antonio BOGGIANO
Buenos Aires, Argentina

Mr. Fritz ENDERLEIN
Akademie für Staats-und Rechtswissenschaft der DDR Institut für Ausländisches Recht und Rechtsvergleichung
Potsdam-Babelsberg, GDR

Prof. Arhyrios A. F. FATOUROS
Faculté de Droit
Saloniki, Greece

Prof. Antonio FERRER-CORREIA
University of Coimbra
Coimbra, Portugal

M. Philippe FOUCHARD
Professeur
Université de Paris II
Talant, France

Prof. Pierre GANNAGE
Doyen de la faculté de droit et de sciences politiques
Université Saint-Joseph
Beyrouth, Lebanon

Prof. Horacio A. GRIGERA NAON
Buenos Aires, Argentina

Prof. B. GROSSFELD
Institut für Ausländisches und Internationales Privat- und Wirtschaftsrecht
Münster, FRG

Mr. Anthony G. GUEST
Professor at the University of London, King's College
Faculty of Laws
London, UK

M. Alain HIRSCH
Professeur
Faculté de Droit de Genève
Genève, Switzerland

Prof. Bernd von HOFFMANN
Universität Trier
Trier, FRG

Prof. A. B. KANSUNMU
Lagos, Nigeria

M. F. E. KLEIN
Professeur
Bâle, Switzerland

Prof. L. KOS-RABCEWICZ-ZUBKOWSKI
President
Canadian Centre of Arbitration
University of Ottawa
Ottawa, Canada

Prof. Ole LANDO
Institute of European Market Law
Copenhagen School of Economics and Business Administration
Copenhagen, Denmark

Prof. Andreas F. LOWENFELD
New York University School of Law
New York, USA

Prof. José Manuel OTERO LASTRES
Decano de la Facultad de Derecho
Universidad de Leon
Leon, Spain

Prof. Adelino da PALMA CARLOS
Lisboa, Portugal

Prof. Reha POROY
Professor
Istanbul, Turkey

Prof. Georg RESS
Director
Institute of European Studies
University of Saarbrücken
Saarbrücken, FRG

* This list is regularly amended. For further information, please contact the Secretariat of the Institute, 38 Cours Albert 1er, 75008 Paris.

Mr. Clive M. SCHMITTHOFF
Editor *Journal of Business Law*
London, UK

Mr. Stanislaw J. SOLTYSINSKI
Professor of Law
Dean of A. Mickiewicz University
School of Law and Administration
Poznan, Poland

Mr. P. A. STEIN
Professor of Civil Procedure
Amsterdam University
Amsterdam, Netherlands

Mr. Evelio VERDERA Y TUELLS
Professeur de Droit Commercial
Directeur de l'Institut de Droit Comparé
a`l'Université de Madrid
Madrid, Spain

Mr. Willem VIS
Professor
New York, USA

Mr. C. C. A. VOSKUIL
Director
T.M.C. Asser Institute
The Hague, Netherlands

B. PRACTITIONERS – PRACTITIONERS AND SCHOLARS

Dr. Antonio O. ADEDE
Senior Legal Officer, Codification Division,
Office of Legal Affairs, United Nations
Secretariat, New York, USA

Mr. S. AMOS WAKO
Nairobi, Kenya

Mr. Cedric BARCLAY
London, UK

Mr. G. P. BARTON
Barrister, Wellington, New Zealand

Mr. A. J. van den BERG
Van Doorne and Sjollema, Advocaten,
Rotterdam, Netherlands

Mr. Piero BERNARDINI
Ente Nazionale Idrocarburi, Roma, Italy

Mr. Luigi BIAMONTI
Roma, Italy

M. Henri BUTTIN
Expert près la Cour d'Appel de Versailles,
Argenteuil, France

Mr. Marcelino CABANAS RODRIGUEZ
Abogado, Madrid, Spain

Mr. H. E. P. COORAY
Hon. Secretary of the Sri Lanka National
Council of the International Chamber of
Commerce, Colombo, Sri Lanka

M. Louis COSTET
Directeur du Service juridique, Régie
Nationale Renault, Boulogne sur Seine, France

Mr. Fernando CRUZ
Lisboa, Portugal

Mr. Arved DERINGER
Professor, Rechtsanwalt, Deringer, Tessin,
Herrmann & Sedemund, Köln, FRG

Mr. Rodrigo ECHENIQUE GORDILLO
Jefe de los Servicios juridicos, Banco Exterior
de España, Madrid, Spain

Mr. Claus-Dieter EHLERMANN
Directeur général, Service juridique des
Communautés Européennes, Bruxelles,
Belgium

M. Jacques EL-HAKIM
Professeur agrégé à la Faculté de Droit,
Avocat, Damas, Syria

Dr. Aly H. ELGHATIT
Cairo, Egypt

Dr. Mario FELDMAN
Buenos Aires, Argentina

Dr. Mario FOLCHI
Buenos Aires, Argentina

Mr. Daniel GARCIA-PITA
Bufete Garrigues, Madrid, Spain

Mr. Enrico GENTILE
Direzione Legale, FIAT S.P.A., Torino, Italy

M. Léon GOFFIN
Professeur, Bruxelles, Belgium

M. Rudolf de GRAFFENRIED
Société de Banque Suisse, Bâle, Switzerland

M. Alfred HUBERT
Directeur, Electrobel, Bruxelles, Belgium

Mr. Rabi KORAL
Avukat, Istanbul, Turkey

M. Hendrik LE PAGE
Conseiller juridique, Agfa-Gevaert N.V.,
Mortsel, Belgium

Mr. Humphrey LLOYD, Q.C.
London, UK

Mr. R. S. LODHA
Lodha & Company, Calcutta, India

Mr. Ghaleb S. MAHMASSANI
Attorney-at-Law, Paris, France

Mr. Habib MALOUCHE
Association professionelle des banques de Tunisie, Tunis, Tunisia

Me Frédéric MARTINET
Martinet, Bataillon, Barberon, Ravaud, Paris, France

M. Lambert MATRAY
Avocat au Barreau de Liège, Ancien Bâtonnier de l'Ordre des Avocats de Liège, Liège, Belgium

Mr. Dara P. MEHTA
Little and Company, Bombay, India

Mr. Marcel A. MEYER
Manager SUNECON, raadgevend ingenieursbureau,
Paramaribo, Surinam

Mr. Renzo MORERA
Avocat à la Cour, Rome, Italy

Dr. Friedrich MOSING
Rechtsanwalt, Wien, Austria

Mr. Yasuharu NAGASHIMA
Nagashima and Ohno, Tokyo, Japan

Mr. Nani A. PALKHIVALA
Director, Tata Sons Limited, Bombay, India

Mr. Gerald POINTON
Herbert Smith & Co., Paris, France

Me Navro RUBINO-SAMMARTANO
Studio Rubino-Sammartano e Associati, Milano, Italy

M. Robert SACRE
Secrétaire général, Sarma Penney Ltd., Bruxelles, Belgium

Mr. Luciano E. SALAZAR
Philippines

Mr. Sven SALEN
Stockholm, Sweden

Me. Ali EL SHALAKHANI
Cairo, Egypt

Mr. R. K. P. SHANKARDASS
Advocate, Supreme Court, New Delhi, India

Mr. Sten SILJESTROM
Chief Legal Advisor, ASEA Koncernkontoret, Stockholm, Sweden

M. Xavier TANDEAU DE MARSAC
Avocat au Barreau de Paris, Cabinet T. de Marsac, Serrero, Popineau & associés, Paris, France

Me Yerim THIAM
Dakar, Senegal

Mr. Vesa VAINIO
Director, Confederation of Finnish Industries, Helsinki, Finland

M. Jean VAN UYTVANCK
Conseiller juridique, Pétrofina S.A., Bruxelles, Belgium

Mr. Robert B. VON MEHREN
Debevoise & Plimpton, New York, USA

Mr. Hans DE VRIES
Foreign Trade Legal Adviser, Philips N.V., Geldrop, The Netherlands

M. Derrick WIDMER
Directeur, Holderbank Management und Beratung AG, Holderbank, Switzerland

CHAPTER II

LIST OF CONTRIBUTORS TO THIS RESEARCH

Argentina
Naón, Horacio Grigera

Australia
Lacher, Stephen

Austria
Melis, Werner
Schinnerer, E.

Belgium
AGFA-Gevaert (Le Page, H.)
CEPANI (Huys, Marcel)
Hubert, Alfred
Le Brun, Jean
Perin, Bernard
van Hecke, G.

Brazil
Bernardes Neto, Horacio
Pinheiro Neto – Avogados (Furquium Filho, Mário)

Bulgaria
Stalev, Zhivko

Canada
Kos-Rabcewicz-Zubkowski, Ludwik

Chile
Friese, Heinz

Colombia
National Committee of Colombia (Martinez Neira, N.H.)

Czechoslovakia
Hanak, Svetozar

Denmark
Gomard, Bernhard

Finland
Erma, Reino
Möller, Gustav

France
Buttin, Henri
Coudert Frères (Paulsson, Jan)
Delvolvé, Jean-Louis
Falque, Dominique
Leducq, Xavier
Pousset, André
Ryvkine, Boris
Sanson, René
Touscoz, Jean
Vedel, Georges

Germany, Fed. Rep. of
Bundesamt für Wehrtechnik und Beschaffung (Lederer, B.)
Bundesminister für das Post- und Fernmeldewesen (Reinke)
Deutscher Ausschuß für das Schiedsgerichtswesen (Böshagen, Fritz/Swoboda, Michael)
Deutsche Bundesbahn
Lau, Emil
Pfaff, Dieter
Sandrock, Otto
Schlafer, Heinz Dieter
Verein deutscher Maschinenbauanstalten; VDMA (Stumpf, Herbert)

Germany (German Democratic Republic)
Strohbach, Heinz
Enderlein, Fritz

Great Britain
Barclay, Cedric
Fletcher, Leonard
Foster, Sir John (†)
Hunter, Robert L. C.
Möllering, J.
Tompkins, W.E.

Hong Kong
Gittins, S. V.

India
Indian Council of Arbitration (Nirwani, S.C.)

Ireland
Abrahamson, Max

Indonesia
Subekti, R.

Italy
Bernardini, Piero
Garone, Giovanni
Morera, Renzo
Recchia, Giorgio
Ribolzi, Cesare
Savarese, Michele
Selvaggi, Carlo

Korea
Cho, Dong Won

Luxembourg
Ahlborn, Henri
Arendt, Ernest
Parquet Général (Edon, N.)

Mexico
Castro, Leonel

Morocco
Bentahila, A.
Meylan, Marc

Netherlands
Buruma, Lely, Magis & Meijer (Langeveld, S.V.)

Nigeria
Ajibola, Bola Adesumbo

Poland
Lopuski, Jan
Popiolek, Wojciech

Saudi Arabia
Falque, Dominique
Bernardini, Piero

Sweden
Dworén, Martin
Westerling, Bengt

Switzerland
Bucher, Eugen
Interfood (Huber, Jean)
Pestalozzi & Gmuer (Karrer, Pierre)
Wenger, Werner
ICC-Enterprises (D. Gutmann)

Syria
El-Hakim, Jacques
Sarkis, Sami

Turkey
Devres, Nezih
Özsunay, Ergun

Uganda
Maiwald, Beate

USA
Coulson, Robert

Yugoslavia
Goldštajn, Aleksandar

IATA
Reifarth, Jürgen

ICC
Leducq, Xavier

ICSID
Bernardini, Piero
Golsong, Herbert

NATO
Buttin, Henri

CHAPTER III

INTRODUCTION, SUMMARY AND CONCLUSIONS

1. RELEVANCE OF THE TOPIC

It was not surprising that business circles as well as practising lawyers and university professors suggested that the Institute of International Business Law and Practice initiate a research study into the specific problems arising from the involvement of state enterprises in international commercial arbitration. The topic is indeed of practical importance; it raises interesting aspects of the law of international business and state relations, and the Institute appears to be well equipped for such a task.

Practical importance: for many years, state enterprises have been participating to a growing extent in international trade. In many socialist countries, be they industrialized as in Eastern Europe or still developing as in other parts of the world, a state monopoly on foreign trade is part of the national economic and legal system. State enterprises are then the exclusive instruments by which such states participate in international commerce. Furthermore, in many developing countries such participation by state enterprises is the result of practical necessities, since often private enterprises in such countries have not yet reached a level which enables them to deal effectively with large international business projects. In industrialized private economy countries state enterprises also have their role of participation in international commerce. If one studies closer the participation of the state in many western countries, one is often surprised to find out that this participation is greater than expected for a variety of reasons and in a variety of ways.

When state enterprises thus participate in international commerce, they are obviously confronted with a desire of their foreign business partners commonly to agree to arbitration as the prevailing technique to be used for settling disputes in international business relations. This is where the challenging legal questions of the topic come in. For state enterprises, both the question of whether and under what circumstances they can or should submit to arbitration, as well as the legal consequences of such a submission both for the arbitration proceedings and the eventual enforcement of awards, raise a number of specific questions and problems *de lege lata* and *de lege ferenda*.

Practical importance and legal interest is illustrated by the collection of cases and the bibliography published at the end of this book. Certain aspects of the topic have also been dealt with by international institutions in recent years: the Arbitration Committee of the International Law Association, in its reports between 1960 and 1978[1] under the Chairmanship of the late Martin Domke, dealt with arbitration between states or government-controlled bodies and foreign-owned business firms; the new Arbitration Committee of the International Law Association, at the ILA Conference in Montreal in 1982, dealt with a report on arbitration between parties from industrialized and less-developed countries prepared by this author, and decided to continue this research which, due to the above-mentioned relevance of state enterprises in developing countries, will deal with certain aspects of our topic. Another illustration of international interest is that, within the framework of the International Council for Commercial Arbitration, a working group of the 1975 International Arbitration Congress in New Delhi also worked on certain aspects of the topic.

If, nevertheless, business circles as well as practising and academic lawyers suggested this research to the Institute of International Business Law and Practice, it was for the reason that this Institute had available sources of information and communication which had not been used before in this context.

2. THE RESEARCH PROJECT AND ITS USE OF THE SPECIFIC SOURCES OF THE INSTITUTE

2.1. Approach and Procedure

Though my former publications and arbitration practice dealing with state enterprises in international commerce and investment gave me a primary interest in the topic in addition to the practical importance and challenging legal questions mentioned above, another important reason for me to accept when I was asked whether I would be prepared to be the general rapporteur for this research project, was the specific advantages offered by the Institute of International Business Law and Practice. This Institute seemed to me indeed especially fit to conduct such a research project. First of all it enjoys the participation of the most eminent international practising lawyers and university professors as well as representatives of the international business community. Secondly, it permits access to the practice of international business relations not only by the participation of persons from the international business community but also through the network of the International Chamber of Commerce, the oldest and most important international organization of the international business community. The channels for this access are, on the one hand, the various commissions, committees and working groups that exist within the ICC and draw their membership from the various national backgrounds and branches of the international business community, and, on the other hand, through the national committees of the ICC that themselves again are often recruited by the business associations and Chambers of Commerce and Industry in their respective countries.

1. See the Reports and Resolutions published in the Proceedings of the ILA Conferences 1960 to 1978.

These additional sources of information and channels of communication available through the Institute proved to be very useful during the conduct of this research project. However, the reader may not be surprised to hear from the general rapporteur that he would have liked to receive even more co-operation, more and more comprehensive contributions, as well as more and more detailed comments, and that he, therefore, is not fully satisfied with the results that could be produced. Anybody who has been engaged in a large research project, especially on an international level, will agree that, for most of the time, the persons best qualified to be sources of information are also under the burden of many other demands and may only be able to invest a limited amount of time and effort on such a research project, even if they agree on its importance. The result is a compromise which one has to accept if one is to be realistic and if the better should not stop the good.

The method used in this research project is described in more detail in Chapter IV, section A, below. Here it may only be pointed out again that the background of this research project as described above and the method chosen on the basis of this background made it preferable to present the publication as it is now. This means in particular that the contributions received have been kept as authentic as possible and that the evaluation of the general rapporteur and his conclusions from the collected information are only presented within this introductory chapter. Thus, the reader can make his own evaluation from the relevant information collected, and in addition may make use of the evaluation by the general rapporteur if he or she so wishes.

2.2. The Meaning of the Term 'State Enterprise'

There is no fixed definition of the term 'state enterprise'. The term is indeed used with at least partly varying meanings in different national, legal and economic contexts as well as by different authors.[2] These variations are partly accidental, partly the result of different political, economic or legal systems, as indicated by the answers received to Question 4 of our questionnaires. The variation of the terminology is also partly intentional to reach certain results regarding specific legal aspects or questions – such as the dispute within the discussion on eventual codes on multinational enterprises whether or not, under specific circumstances state enterprises can or should also be considered to be multinational enterprises.[3]

Since there is no fixed definition of the term 'state enterprise' and since none of the varying definitions can claim general acceptance, the approach of this research project is a simple one: I have defined the term in a rather wide sense

2. This is part of the general problem regarding the identification of state-parties in international arbitration: see Böckstiegel, 'Specific Problems of International Arbitration between States and Private Enterprises' in *Proceedings, Vth International Arbitration Congress*, New Delhi, 1975, C, III, 3, 4, f.

3. By now the view seems to have prevailed that state enterprises can also be transnational corporations to which the code should apply: the UN draft expressly includes 'state-owned or state-controlled enterprises' (Doc. E/C. 10/79), the ILO Tripartite Declaration expressly includes 'enterprises, whether they are of public, mixed or private ownership' (§6).

in order to cover indirect state participation in international business relations as widely as possible in the collection of information and possibly also in its evaluation:

> 'State Enterprise' in this research project is understood to be any commercial enterprise predominantly owned or controlled by the state or by state institutions, with or without separate legal personality.

Every contributor to this research project and to this publication was given that definition in advance and therefore it may be assumed that the information and comments received and presented in this publication concern state enterprises as understood by that definition. This, of course, does not mean that one can disregard the many legal forms given to state enterprises in various national laws, when concrete legal evaluations are at stake, as Mitrovic rightly pointed out in the discussion of the Stockholm Colloquium. The results of the research show that, for many aspects of arbitration involving state enterprises in the defined broad sense, one may have to distinguish between various types of state enterprises concerning the applicability of certain rules and laws on the basis of specific criteria.

It should also be pointed out that this research only collected information on state enterprises created by one particular state. As Pierre Lalive has rightly pointed out in a communication within this project, there seems to exist an increasing number of joint 'international state enterprises' created by several states with or without separate legal personality, limited or not.[4] They give rise to specific considerations and problems not discussed in this study so that the findings of this research, although sometimes also applicable to them, cannot be applied to such international state enterprises without additional screening.

3. PRACTICE OF STATE ENTERPRISES REGARDING ARBITRATION

3.1. Legal Restrictions upon Submission to Arbitration

The practice of state enterprises with regard to arbitration obviously depends on the existence or non-existence of legal restrictions upon submission to arbitration. Therefore, before examining what actually is the practice of state enterprises in this context, the information collected on such legal restrictions will be considered here.

This order of examination also seems advisable, because it is a well-known fact of international contract negotiations that state enterprises, in their attempt to reach the jurisdiction of their own national courts, often claim that legal restrictions stop them from agreeing to international arbitration. It is an equally well known fact that such a claim, if examined more closely, often proves to be incorrect or at least applicable only to the state itself or public

4. *See* Libbrecht, *Entreprises à caractère juridiquement international* (Sijthoff, Leiden 1972).

entities, but not, however, to most state enterprises. If at all, only those state enterprises in the form of public entities are subject to restrictions in certain states, while the great majority of state enterprises in the form of private law companies or corporations are normally not at all subject to the restrictions and therefore free to submit to arbitration in their participation in international commercial activities.

The material received reflects the different attitudes taken by national legislators towards arbitration in general and towards the submission of the state and its institutions and enterprises to arbitration in particular.

As far as the industrialized socialist countries of Eastern Europe are concerned, there is of course a state monopoly of foreign trade which is exercised by the well known foreign trade state enterprises, and there is not only no restriction on their submission to arbitration, but, on the contrary, arbitration is the exclusive method of dispute settlement in business relations with other socialist countries and also the standard method in contracts with business partners in non-socialist countries.

As far as the industrialized private economy countries of Western Europe are concerned, the above-mentioned distinction between public entities and state enterprises incorporated in private law comes into play. While there are practically no restrictions for private law companies, even if they are predominantly owned or controlled by the state, a variety of restrictions exists on the submission of the state or public entities to arbitration.

No restrictions seem to exist in Austria and Great Britain, Italy, the Netherlands and Switzerland. In Belgium[5] and Luxembourg, public entities are in principle forbidden to agree to arbitration agreements, either in an internal or an international contract. Exceptions to this rule can only be made by law; that is, by a stipulation which allows arbitration to some special public legal entity. No such exception by law seems to exist in Luxembourg. In Belgium an exception has been made for instance in Article 6 of the law setting up the Office National du Ducroire. And the Belgian state itself, according to Article 1676, is allowed to agree to arbitration where an international treaty makes provisions for arbitration proceedings, such as Article 2 of the European Convention on Arbitration to which Belgium adheres and the World Bank Convention on Arbitration in Investment Disputes between States and Foreign Enterprises.

In France the state and public entities need specific permission to submit to arbitration, but it is generally admitted that this refers only to internal contracts, and that, for contracts in international business, submission to arbitration is permitted. This is due to the famous decision in 1966 of the Cour de Cassation to the effect that the prohibition of submission to arbitration was not valid with regard to international contracts. The recent changes to French arbitration law in 1980 (national arbitration) and 1981 (international arbitration) do not seem to have brought any changes in this respect. In the Federal Republic of Germany, due to a law of 1933, submission of the state itself and its

5. In addition to the material received in this research *see also* Storme, 'L'Arbitrage entre Personnes de Droit Public et Persones de Droit Privé', *Revue de l'Arbitrage* (1978) 113 ff.

public entities to arbitration requires the consent of the Minister of Finances. Otherwise there are no restrictions, especially none for state enterprises in the form of private law companies or corporations.

Finally, though in Finland there is no restriction on submission to arbitration, public entities keep the option to go to court in spite of the arbitration agreement. In that context it should be noted that the European Convention on Commercial Arbitration of April 21, 1961, expressly provides in its Article II for the right of legal persons in public law to resort to arbitration, but also permits a declaration of limitation of that principle for ratifying states.

Looking at industrialized private economy countries outside Europe, we have to note first that in the United States the federal government and some state governments often contend that they are not authorized to submit to arbitration while other states and most local governments and public authorities are authorized to arbitrate. No restriction seems to exist with regard to enterprises in the form of private law companies or corporations which are predominantly owned or controlled by the state. No restrictions are reported with regard to Canada and Australia.

The information received from the Third World varies considerably.

Among the Arab countries[6] Saudi Arabia is well known for restricting arbitration clauses in government contracts though that does not seem to apply to private companies which are owned or controlled only by the government. But even the well known decision of the Council of Ministers prohibiting arbitration for government agencies allowed an exception in 'cases where the state shall grant a concession and in doing so finds the utmost advantage in including the arbitration clause in such concession'. The new Saudi Arabian Decree of June 1983 has brought about a liberalization regarding arbitration which has already had its effect in practice as illustrated by a number of new authorized arbitration clauses and by the statement of Sheik Yamani during the conference on the occasion of the 60th anniversary of the ICC Court of Arbitration in Paris in October 1983. This indication of a greater flexibility is confirmed by the negotiating position which the Arab countries take in the dialogue on a multilateral investment protection treaty between the Arab League and the European Community. Other Arab states like Morocco and Syria have no restrictions for state institutions in general submitting to arbitration.

A traditionally difficult region for arbitration is Latin-America. In Argentina no specific restrictions exist for state enterprises, but of course the general limitations for submission to arbitration also apply to them. We find a similar state of the law in Brazil, while in Chile fields in which all state enterprises may agree to arbitration are enumeratively listed in a special decree. Mexico, of all the Latin-American states the most liberal country for international arbitration, confirms that position with regard to state enterprises where no restrictions exist for their submission to arbitration.

A rather varied picture is also presented from reports from other regions of

6. For a survey of contractual practice and dispute settlement in business relations with partners in the Arab countries *see* Böckstiegel, *Vertragspraxis und Streiterledigung im Wirtschaftsverkehr mit arabischen Staaten*, Vol. 2 of the series of the German Institute of Arbitration (Cologne 1981).

the world. No restrictions exist in Turkey. None exists also in Nigeria where, as is well known from the cement cases, the state itself also agrees to arbitration in international contracts. No restrictions are found in Indonesia and Korea, while in India governments sometimes prescribe specific methods for dispute settlement by administrative or legal orders.

The general impression from the reporting on eventual restrictions on state enterprises submitting to arbitration is that the full picture might not be seen by looking at the written law by itself, since someties administrative measures may still lead to restrictions while in other countries courts may apply the written restriction to only national contracts and admit submission to arbitration in international commercial contracts.

3.2. The Practice of Submitting to Arbitration

It has been seen above – as for instance in the case of France – that even legal restrictions on submission to arbitration may in fact be interpreted not to apply to international commercial contracts. Generally, however, legal restrictions, if existing, present limits on the submission of state enterprises to arbitration. The question to be dealt with now is whether state enterprises – within these limits of the law – actually make use of the possibility to submit to arbitration and to what extent.

A review of the information collected in this context demonstrates the fundamental difference between national and international contracts. While for national contracts it is often indicated that submission to arbitration is not usual, for international contracts concluded by the state enterprise with foreign partners, on the other hand, arbitration is reported to be in fact accepted to a great extent. This is in conformity with the impression one obtains from the general international contract practice of state enterprises and from reporting in the publications. The negotiating situation seems to be that state enterprises are primarily pressing for the jurisdiction of the courts of their respective home states or at least arbitration bodies within their home states more often than private enterprises, while, on the contrary, their foreign partners seem to be pressing not to choose such courts or arbitration bodies of the home state of the state enterprise. The position of the state enterprises seems to be to a certain extent influenced by the position often taken by states themselves when they, for reasons of sovereignty and national prestige, consider they should not accept foreign jurisdiction. The position of private foreign enterprises seems to be mainly due to the consideration that referring the decision on contractual questions to the national courts or arbitration bodies of the other state would bring about a possible collision of interest for the judges or arbitrators, because they have to decide a case between, on one side, the state that grants them salaries, advancement, social security and has many ways of exerting pressure upon them, and, on the other side, a foreign company often coming from an entirely different social and legal system and towards which they may have an approach of at least indifference. Though certainly the great majority of judges and national arbitrators will nevertheless take up the case with the greatest impartiality, the mere possibility of this not being so is reason enough for foreign private enterprises to try to avoid the jurisdiction of the national courts or national arbitration bodies of the contracting state enterprise.

Thus, since neither national jurisdiction nor national arbitration does not often seem to be an acceptable solution to either one of the parties, the natural solution is to agree on an international arbitral tribunal. This seems to be the major reason behind the reporting in this research project that, to a much larger extent than in national contracts, in international contracts state enterprises accept arbitration by international arbitral tribunals.

The clearest picture is again presented by the socialist countries. For state enterprises in countries belonging to the Council for Mutual Economic Assistance (CMEA) – and they of course have a monopoly for foreign trade in those countries – submitting to arbitration is an absolutely common practice. Contracts between enterprises from different CMEA states submit exclusively to arbitration due to a respective compulsory provision in the generally used conditions of contract between them. With regard to contracts between state enterprises from CMEA countries and partners from non-CMEA countries, submission to arbitration is also a general practice though it is not obligatory.

A survey of the answers received from industrialized private economy countries presents a less homogeneous picture. The hesitancy to submit to arbitration in national contracts may be of less interest for the international business community. With regard to international contracts, only state enterprises in Belgium, Canada and Denmark seldom seem to agree to arbitration. This is also the case in the Netherlands, except that arbitration agreements are more common in construction contracts. In Sweden the approach seems to be rather pragmatic. While at least the state and public entities try strongly to avoid submitting to arbitration, they have nevertheless in some very important contracts in fact submitted to arbitration. For most other industrialized private economy countries the information received shows that state enterprises often submit to arbitration. This can be seen in the answers received from Australia, Austria, Finland, France, Federal Republic of Germany, Great Britain, Ireland, Italy, Luxembourg, Switzerland and the United States.

Information received from Third World countries describes the submission of state enterprises to arbitration either as 'seldom' (Argentina, Brazil Morocco, Turkey) or as 'often' (Chile, India, Korea, Mexico, Nigeria and Syria). From other sources,[7] for a report I prepared for the Montreal Conference of the International Law Association in 1982[8] on 'Arbitration between Parties from Industrialized and Less-Developed Countries' in consultation with members of the respective international ILA committee, it was found that international commercial arbitration was the generally preferred

7. *See also* Tiewul and Tsegah, 'Arbitration and the Settlement of Commercial Disputes: A Selective Survey of African Practice' 241CLQ (1975) 393 ff., 406 ff., McLaughlin, 'Arbitration and Developing Countries', *The International Lawyer* (1979) 211 ff.

8. Reprinted as the Report of the ILA Committee on International Commercial Arbitration in Proceedings of the Montreal 1982 Conference of the International Law Association.

instrument for the settlement of disputes at least for larger contracts. A recent example is that on May 18, 1981, the government of the United Arab Republic recommended to all state institutions and state enterprises to include in their contracts with foreign partners an arbitration clause referring to the new Cairo International Commercial Arbitration Centre (CICAC).[9]

The general impression is, therefore, that, in a great majority of states, at least in international contracts, arbitration has been accepted as an effective means of settling disputes arising out of business contracts. It is not easy to make out the reasons behind the obvious reluctance of state enterprises in the other states. One may wonder whether the negative attitude in such cases has to do with a certain nationalism on the side of those who under all circumstances insist on agreeing on the jurisdiction of their own countries' ordinary courts. Perhaps it is also true that state functionaries just feel more comfortable with ordinary courts. Perhaps there is also a kind of shyness towards arbitration on the part of state enterprises, because they feel the public may not understand or accept a movement away from the ordinary courts towards private sector dispute settlement instead.

In addition, President Bellet, in the discussion of the Stockholm Colloquium, indicated that the hesitations of state employees to submit to international commercial arbitration may be due to language problems, the costs of arbitration in comparison to the services of their own courts which were available to the state practically free of charge, and to the hesitation they have in taking fast decisions in arbitration on their own responsibility without always being able to receive a long series of approvals from their superiors. The latter point may conform with the experience of other arbitrators active in this field. It often happens that, in cases where an amicable settlement would be considered to be the best solution, even if the terms achievable in such an amicable settlement are obviously better for the state enterprise than the most provable result of an arbitration award, the state employees may not agree, because then they would have taken responsibility and have to explain that to their superiors, while otherwise in the 'dictated' solution by an arbitration award their own personal responsibility is not involved.[10]

Finally, the approach of state enterprises seems to be not too far different from that known for private enterprises in international trade. There is a certain preference for one's own jurisdiction which one knows and with which one feels comfortable. Since that is also the approach of the other contractual party in the negotiations, unless the negotiating power of one side is extremely strong, the compromise most often reached is to submit to international arbitration which is neutral and does not give an advantage to either side in case of a dispute. Though the negotiating power of at least those state enterprises that are in the position of buyers has been rather strong in the difficult and most competitive world market of recent years, nevertheless, it

9. The Centre will normally apply the UNCITRAL Arbitration Rules.

10. *See also* Ribolzi, 'The choice and appointment of board of arbitrators in disputes concerning public works of local public bodies' in *Arbitrage Commercial, Essais in Memoriam Eugenio Minoli* (Torino 1974), 425 ff.

seems that the compromise on arbitration is more often than not the result of the respective negotiations. This conclusion is not only confirmed by the answers received within this research project but also from the experience that can be obtained from the majority of large international tenders where, in many cases, right from the beginning, the conditions of tender already contain an arbitration clause.

3.3. The Kind of Arbitration Accepted

If state enterprises agree to arbitration, there is of course a wide scale of kinds of arbitration from which they may choose. The information collected[10] indicates that this rather wide scale is in fact made use of though clear preferences can be seen.

First of all, as in contract negotiations between private companies, state enterprises seem also to have a preference for trying to choose a national arbitration machinery in their own country if that is available and if they can reach that in the contract negotiations. This is first of all true for the socialist countries of Eastern Europe with their specific national foreign trade arbitration courts. These are generally chosen for contracts between foreign trade state enterprises that both come from CMEA countries. If foreign trade state enterprises conclude contracts with partners from non-CMEA countries, especially from western private economy countries, they might still prefer their own national arbitration machinery, but do not seem to insist upon it if – as is normally the case – the western company is not ready to accept a national arbitration institution in the home country of the contractual partner. The foreign trade state enterprises of Eastern Europe will then also agree to the kind of arbitration most favoured elsewhere, especially that of the International Chamber of Commerce where indeed a great many disputes from East-West trade appear.

Outside the socialist countries there also exist national arbitration machineries which are either primarily preferred in negotiations and at least sometimes actually chosen in contracts by state enterprises. This seems to be the case in Austria, Finland, the Federal Republic of Germany, Great Britain, India, Ireland, Mexico, the Netherlands, Nigeria, Switzerland and the United States. Some of these national arbitration machineries are also sometimes chosen as a neutral administered arbitration by the foreign contractual partner including state enterprises. This is especially true for the arbitration rules administered in Zurich, Vienna and Stockholm.

The kind of arbitration most often reported to be chosen by state enterprises is that provided by the International Chamber of Commerce. This, of course, is not surprising because that arbitration is also the one most often agreed upon and which has the greatest number of actual arbitration proceedings in international business relations in general between private companies. Statistics show that ICC arbitration is also often chosen by states themselves if they enter into international business or investment contracts. This picture is confirmed by the reports received within this research project where ICC arbitration is mentioned as being chosen by state enterprises in their international contracts more often than any other arbitration.[11]

The second most mentioned kind of arbitration in relation to state enterprises is *ad-hoc* arbitration. State enterprises in Argentina, Austria, Brazil, Finland, France, Great Britain, India, Ireland, Mexico, Morocco, Nigeria, Switzerland and the United States are reported as having chosen *ad-hoc* arbitration.

Though only a few reports (from Australia, Great Britain, Poland and Yugoslavia) mention that state enterprises also agree to the specific arbitration machineries created for specific branches of business, such as textiles or sugar, it might well be that this is a wider practice than is shown from the information available.

In view of the relatively short period of time for which the UNCITRAL Arbitration Rules have existed, it is not surprising that they have not often been mentioned as being accepted by state enterprises. Nevertheless, reports from Austria, the German Democratic Republic, Korea and Morocco refer especially to these UNCITRAL Rules which might well play a more important role in the future.

Finally, it should be mentioned that the research that has proved a problem of information also exists in the context of arbitration and state enterprises as well as in international commercial arbitration in general. Since both the agreement to arbitrate as well as the actual arbitration procedures are mostly confidential, one could not expect much information on actual arbitration awards. Nevertheless, the respective question 1.4. of the Questionnaire produced some references to a number of published awards which had not been known before. They have been included in the collection of cases in this book.

3.4. Practical Problems Experienced

When one is trying to find out about specific practical problems that have been experienced in arbitration with state enterprises, one has to be aware of course that all those problems that appear in international commercial arbitration in general may also appear here. They are not given any consideration within the scope of this research, unless they appear to be of greater relevance in our context.

Furthermore, some of the problems experienced in arbitration with state enterprises are of course those that, in view of their specific relevance, are dealt with in other sections of this publication in more detail. Thus, with regard to the problems of submission to arbitration, the determination of the applicable law, dealing with acts of the home state as *force majeure* or the enforcement of arbitration awards, reference can be made here to the appropriate chapters of this book and, in addition, to the panel contribution and the discussion at the Stockholm Colloquium reprinted in this book.

Other practical problems reported as having been specifically experienced in

11. In that context *see* Böckstiegel, 'Arbitration on Disputes between states and Private Enterprises in the International Chamber of Commerce', 59AJIL (1965) 579 ff.

arbitration with state enterprises nevertheless appear from the information collected as follows.

A problem that was mentioned several times may be characterized by the comment from Mr. Barclay of Great Britain of arbitration involving state enterprises as being 'very slow moving'. His, as well as the parallel comments from other sources, seem to incidate that arbitration involving state enterprises will often tend to be slower than arbitration between private enterprises due to the special structure of public administrations and their complicated way of reaching decisions therein. There is no obvious reason to suppose that this problem of undue delay with state enterprises would be of less importance in ordinary court litigation where such enterprises are involved, especially since one may have to go through three instances of state courts before getting a final judgment.

A problem also mentioned several times and confirmed by experience in arbitration with state enterprises is that it is often much more difficult to reach an amicable settlement with state enterprises. The fact that very often an amicable settlement might be more favourable in view of the expense of a prolonged arbitration and also in view of the unknown outcome of an arbitration procedure seems to be overridden by the problems of personal responsibility within public entities be they themselves involved in the arbitration or the controlling state enterprise. Quite often the individuals in charge in state administrations may prove less ready to take responsibility for decisions than one might find in private enterprises. The civil servant may consider it as less risky for his own position to have to accept the final decision of an arbitral tribunal than taking upon himself the responsibility of a decision for a certain amicable compromise and the need to convince the rest of the state administration that this was a good choice. Furthermore, as Pierre Lalive rightly pointed out, a somewhat similar reason for the difficulty in reaching an amicable settlement is that the only persons capable of deciding (president of the state enterprise, ministers, etc.) are often not fully informed by those in charge of the case (whether public officials or lawyers). The latter are tempted to give biased accounts of the arbitration proceedings in order to protect their responsibility or to overestimate their own forensic achievements.

Pieter Sanders, in the discussion at the Stockholm Colloquium, rightly pointed out that renegotiation of long-term contracts might often be also more difficult in contracts and arbitration with state enterprises.

Other problems seem to be less relevant, but should nevertheless be mentioned here so that they might be considered and taken care of in future cases.

It is sometimes observed that arbitrators named by state enterprises were often biased and acted under the instructions of the respective administration. In view of their difficult psychological or political position, admitting dissenting opinions might be a useful protection device.

One correspondent observed that arbitrators named by state enterprises from developing countries sometimes lack full knowledge of the technique of arbitration.

Quite often a state enterprise seems to have more problems in making, or at least seems to need more time to make, the necessary advance payment for the arbitration procedure.

A rather specific situation exists in Australia where at least for arbitration on the national level the national rules sometimes lead to certain disadvantages for the private partner in relation to the state enterprise.

4. DETERMINATION OF THE APPLICABLE LAW

When, in relation to arbitration, judges, arbitrators or authors speak of the 'applicable law' they do not always mean the same thing. The term is sometimes used rather indifferently with regard to three separate questions: What is the applicable procedural law? What are the applicable conflict of laws rules? What is the applicable substantive law? All three of these questions have their definitive relevance in any kind of international commercial arbitration, though that relevance is sometimes over-estimated in view of the fact that in the practice of international arbitration – at least on the basis of the experience of this author – the majority of cases is decided exclusively on the interpretation of contracts and the relevance of trade usages so that very little depends on the question of the applicable law. On the other hand, of course, in those cases where the applicable law actually is of relevance for the result of the arbitration, the arbitrators often have a difficult task in deciding that question. In the discussion at the Stockholm Colloquium, Lando, Ermgard and Riedinger considered the unpredictablity of the applicable law as a major obstacle or difficulty in international arbitrations with state enterprises. Lando, in that context, referred to efforts within the ICC to improve that situation, at least within ICC arbitrations.

In this research on the role of state enterprises in international commercial arbitration, it is obvious that only the special aspects of the question of the applicable law that arise if one of the parties is indeed a state enterprise can be considered.

Before going into such special aspects, in order not to lose the right perspective of the whole matter, it should be noted that the results of the research confirm what those active in this kind of arbitration will also find as their own personal experience, that normally the applicable law in arbitration with state enterprises can and will be found in applying the same criteria as are used for contracts and disputes between private enterprises in international commercial arbitration. Only in a minority of cases and in relation to certain aspects of the disputes, therefore, will additional specific criteria have to be considered because one party is a state enterprise.

4.1. The Applicable Procedural Law

The only specific aspect for state enterprises with regard to the procedural law of an international commercial arbitration could be that in those few states – like Saudi Arabia – where national law contains restrictions with regard to the law applicable to contracts by the state or its institutions, this restriction on the applicable law might be considered also to restrict applicable procedural law. In other words, in cases where submission to arbitration is permissible and nevertheless the restriction regarding the applicable law applies, the general rules for the determination of the applicable procedural law might be influenced by this specific consideration. The extent of this influence obviously depends on the present state of the law and arbitration practice for determining the procedural law.[12]

First it has to be pointed out that the parties are granted a wide autonomy in the choice of the procedural law applicable to their international commercial arbitrations. The procedural problems reported by Eisemann in the discussion of the Stockholm Colloquium as well as general experience indicate that it may be wise for the parties to exercise that autonomy. This autonomy is sometimes exercised by specific contractual clauses expressly determining which procedural law the arbitrators should apply; more often it is used in an indirect way by the parties choosing the arbitration rules of one of the well-known international arbitration institutions. These rules contain a regulation on the procedural law the arbitrators have to apply. It may well be again that the regulation is rather flexible and leaves the choice of the procedural law to the parties or, if the parties fail to exercise their choice, to the arbitrators. Thus, for instance, Article 11 of the ICC Arbitration Rules provides that the proceedings shall be governed by 'any rules which the parties (or, failing them, the arbitrator) may settle, and whether or not a reference is thereby made to a municipal procedural law to be applied to the arbitration'. Article 11, which came into force with the new version of the arbitration rules of 1975, is of specific interest because it illustrates an important change from the former Article 16 which, under the influence of the 1952 Sienna resolution of the Institut de Droit International, followed the doctrine that the arbitrators had to apply the procedural law of the seat of arbitration. Thus the new Article 11 gives much wider freedom to the arbitrators to determine the procedure, a trend which is also accepted in *ad hoc* arbitration and in the UNCITRAL Arbitration Rules. In fact, as this author has been able to demonstrate in his report[13] on the UNCITRAL Arbitration Rules to the 1982 Stockholm Symposium on 'International Commercial Arbitration', organized by the Stockholm Chamber of Commerce, the American Arbitration Association, the USSR Chamber of Commerce and Industry and UNCITRAL, they contain a presumption in favour of freedom from national arbitration law to the effect that only mandatory provisions of the applicable national arbitration law have to be respected by the arbitrators. 'Mandatory', in the context of international arbitration would have to be understood in the sense of '*ordre public international*', as Pierre Lalive pointed out in a comment.

It is only in the context of such mandatory procedural regulations that

12. *See also*: Delaume, 'State Contracts and Transnational Arbitration', 75AJIL (1981) 784, 790 ff.

13. Böckstiegel, 'The Relationship between the UNCITRAL-Arbitration Rules and the National Law Applicable to the Arbitration', not yet published in the original version, but published in German in RIW (1982) 706 ff.

specific rules regarding the involvement of state enterprises in international commercial arbitration may have to be considered by arbitrators. Two conditions therefore have to be fulfilled: (1) the respective regulations of the home state of the state enterprise have to be considered as part of the 'applicable' law; (2) they have to be considered as 'mandatory'. Now, these conditions are easier stated in the abstract than applied in practice. Since every national legislator determines by himself and autonomously not only which provisions of his arbitration law are mandatory, but also to which cases and activities within the range of his sovereignty they shall apply, it may well be that mandatory provisions of several national laws claim to be applicable to a certain extent, even if the parties have chosen to submit the arbitration to the law of some other country. Such cases may arise with regard to any activity or part of the procedure on the territory and therefore under the sovereignty of a state other than the state whose law of procedure has been chosen as the applicable law for the arbitration. In such a way mandatory regulations of the national law of the place of arbitration may be a basis for the setting aside of the award. Eventual interim or conservatory measures can only be requested from national courts subject to mandatory provisions of the state to which the jurisdictional authority belongs, and can only be effected by the arbitrators subject to the mandatory provisions of the arbitration law they are obliged to apply. The taking of evidence in a third country may be subject to mandatory rules of that country. Specifically with regard to state enterprises, national law restrictions on the submission to arbitration will be indirectly relevant for the jurisdiction of the arbitral tribunal, since that jurisdiction depends on the arbitration agreements which in its turn depends on the capacity of both parties to submit to arbitration. On the other hand, in that context, though such restrictions will generally have to be considered as mandatory, that does not always exclude the arbitrators from accepting their jurisdiction in an international commercial arbitration. As we have seen above, in section 3.1, most national law restrictions for submission to arbitration only apply to the state and public entities and are not applicable if the state enterprise has the legal form of a private law company or corporation. Even more so, where the state or one of its public entities have accepted an arbitration clause, it is considered as part of international public policy that they cannot later claim that they could not submit to arbitration due to their own national laws.[14]

Finally, it should be mentioned that in the *Aramco*[15] and *Texaco/Libya*[16] cases the arbitrators held that the arbitration procedure was directly governed by international law. Only in exceptional circumstances will this solution have to be considered for arbitration with state enterprises.

14. *See* 'The arbitration award' reported by Derains in *Revue de l'arbitrage* (1973) 145 and accepted also by Goldman in *Clunet* (1979) 483.

15. *Saudi Arabia* v. *Aramco*, Award of August 23, 1958, 27, 117, 135.

16. Award of January 19, 1977, 104 *Clunet* (1977) 350, 3ILM (1978) 17.

4.2. The Applicable Conflict of Law Rules

The primary question on the way to determine the applicable substantive law is, of course, which are the applicable conflict of laws rules. For even the extent of party autonomy is subject to these rules. Here we enter a most disputed region of international commercial arbitration. The reason behind this insecurity is chiefly that the international arbitrator has no, or at least a much less intensive, connection with the 'seat' of the arbitration than judges to the forum of national courts. Judges will normally have to apply the private international law of the state to which the court belongs, in other words the *lex fori*. Application of the private international law of the seat of the arbitration is only one of the possible solutions in international arbitration. Other often more adequate solutions are the application of conflict of laws rules determined by comparative law methods or the application of conflict of laws principles of the national law which the arbitrators have found to be applicable for the procedure and which do not necessarily have to be the law of the seat of arbitration.

The information received during this research confirms the impression that, in international commercial arbitration involving state enterprises, the same principles are normally applied to solve conflicts of laws as are applied in international commercial arbitration between private parties. However, a few specific considerations should be pointed out.

Stalev (Bulgaria), in a communication to the questionnaire supplemented by a communication submitted in October 1983, points out in this context that the state enterprise is more closely connected with the respective state than any other person of private law and that this may have relevance on determining the applicable law determining personal status. He also feels that, with regard to the law applicable to the contract, the same conflict rules are to be applied to both private and state enterprises. The observation by Bernardini (Italy) goes in another direction that, in 'state contracts', there is a tendency to alter to a certain extent traditional principles of private international law and, in the absence of an explicit and legally enforceable choice of law pointing to a different legal system, to apply the national law of the state to which the state enterprise belongs. Similarly El-Hakim (Syria) points out that in his country administrative enterprises usually consider the signing of a contract with them as implying a reference to Syrian law. These observations are in some contradiction to the majority of answers received which point out that the normal principles of private international law, as exercised in contracts between private companies, are also applied to contracts involving state enterprises. This majority view is in line with recent views by Dupuy and Pierre Lalive.[17]

In part the difference of evaluation may be due to a distinction raised by Leducq (France) that the French judge may determine the applicable law in different ways for private law contracts on one side and public contracts on the

17. Dupuy in the *Texaco Award op. cit.* Lalive in *UNIDROIT, New Directions in International Trade*, Vol. 2, p. 750 ff.

other side and that he might accept a presumption for the state enterprise's national law in the case of the public contract. My own conclusion from international doctrine and practice would be that, for what in a state is considered as a public contract, the solution is normally that certain regulations of the public law of that state may well have to be applied. However, this does not mean that only the law of that state has to be applied, but that the law generally applicable to the contract may well still be determined in the usual way for international commercial arbitration. This usual method is characterized by the three choices mentioned in the beginning of this chapter.

Two negative conclusions are still important in that context. There is no indication that an international arbitral tribunal, especially if its seat is outside the home state of the state enterprise, has to apply the conflict of laws rules of that home state of the state enterprise. If therefore the law of that home state contains a regulation to the effect that for certain state contracts only the substantive law of that state may be applied, the arbitral tribunal is not bound by that national conflict of laws rule. If, therefore, in a contract between the state enterprise and its foreign partner, no choice of law provision is included, the arbitral tribunal is in no way bound to apply this national conflict of laws rule of the home state of the state enterprise and can still determine the applicable substantive law by the usual methods applied in international commercial arbitration.

The second negative conclusion refers to those cases where the arbitration clause in the contract does not determine the seat of the arbitral tribunal so that the seat will, in case of a conflict, be later only determined either by the arbitrators or by an arbitral institution according to its arbitration rules. In such a case it does not seem permissible to determine the applicable substantive law of the contract on the basis of the *lex fori* of that seat of arbitration, because that would mean that the parties – not knowing of course which seat might be determined later – would have no possibility of finding out the applicable substantive law while performing the contract. For that large number of contracts in which the seat of arbitration is not determined in the contract itself, therefore, the applicable substantive law should not be determined on the basis of the *lex fori*, but on the basis of the other methods established in international commercial arbitration. The comparative law method might be of good service here, either bilaterally trying to establish common principles of the conflict of laws rules of the home laws of the two contractual parties or, if that does not help, multilaterally trying to establish common conflict of laws principles between major legal systems. First of all, however, every effort should be made to trace at least an indirect indication from the contract or its background to find the conflict of laws rules which seem best fit in the interest of both parties and the performance of the contract.

4.3. The Applicable Substantive Law

4.3.1. Choice of Law by the Contractual Parties

For arbitration involving state enterprises, the most important source for determining the applicable substantive law is an eventual choice of law expressed by the contractual parties.

First of all, the information collected by this research definitely confirms that arbitration tribunals as well as national courts, in case they have to deal with the matter, will respect a choice of law by the parties and that the involvement of the state enterprise will not alter that principle.

Whether the parties have chosen a specific substantive law to rule their contract, therefore, depends on the wording and the interpretation of each particular contract that the arbitrators have to deal with. An express choice has to be respected, be it for the national law of one of the parties or be it for some law neutral to both parties – a compromise often found in contractual practice also involving state enterprises.

Those familiar with the reality of negotiating will know that sometimes a state enterprise, be it a separate legal entity or not from the state, may find it more difficult than a private enterprise to agree to some foreign law as governing the contract. Though not legally restricted, they may nevertheless for reasons of national prestige or to avoid possible national political issues prefer not to accept a foreign law. In such cases either by open or silent consent the question of the applicable law may not be raised at all in the contract or even in the contract negotiations. In such circumstances the arbitrators may nevertheless sometimes find certain indications from other provisions of the contract or from the contract negotiations pointing to one specific national law. This situation is also common to international contracts between private enterprises.

The picture of contractual practice presented in the information collected by this research shows that no single pattern can be found in choice of law clauses in contracts with state enterprises. First of all it appears again that obviously the negotiating power of the parties may have a strong influence and may make it possible for one of the two parties to follow its 'homeward trend' by successfully having a choice of law for its own national law introduced into the contract. There are more cases in favour of a state enterprise frequently insisting on the inclusion of its own national law. However, information has also been received to the effect that the home law of the private enterprise is often chosen by an express clause in the contract. If the negotiating power of neither of the parties is not so overwhelming that neither can have its own national law chosen in the contract, the normal compromise seems to be a law neutral to both parties. The choice of that law, it has been indicated, may well be influenced by certain objective criteria for the feasibility of reaching satisfactory solutions from that law for the specific object of the contract and by the subjective standpoint of the parties. If both parties have one common language, such as English or French, they will most probably also choose a law written in that language. If both parties belong to the same legal system such as the common law or civil law systems, they might prefer to choose a neutral law also from that system. If neither of such common denominators exists or is at least considered as relevant, the law of countries well known for their political neutrality such as Switzerland, Austria or Sweden seems to be more often chosen than other national laws.

A much wider variety of choice of choice of law clauses is found in contractual practice if a state enterprise concluding the contract does not take the form of a private law company or corporation but is a public entity of the state or even the state itself. On the basis of research done some years ago on 'the state as contractual partner to foreign private enterprises',[18] and on the basis of the information collected during this research, choice of law provisions are found in contractual practice between such state entities and foreign private enterprises referring:

(1) to the national law of state enterprise;
(2) to the national law of the home country of the private enterprise;
(3) to the national law of a third country;
(4) to two systems of national law;
(5) to a national law and in addition to the 'principle of good will and good faith';
(6) to a national law in combination with 'the general principles of law and justice';
(7) to public international law either explicitly or implied;
(8) to the principles of law common to the national legal systems of the contractual partners;
(9) to 'the principles of law recognized by civilized nations';
(10) exclusively to the contract itself, possibly in addition to *bona fides*;
(11) to legal principles or combinations of legal principles which go beyond any specific category;
(12) to the arbitrators themselves asking them to act as 'amiable compositeurs' or decide *ex aequo et bono*.

This list of categories of choices of law provisions in contracts between state entities and foreign private enterprises by no means mentions all variations existing in such contracts. In addition, further qualifications may make the arbitrator's job even more difficult such as putting several different choices of law in an order of priority and subsidiarity.

In exceptional cases, an example being Saudi Arabia, not all state enterprises, but public entities of the state may be forbidden to choose any foreign law to govern the contract with foreign enterprises. The information received within this research as well as that collected for a recent publication of the German Institute of Arbitration, edited by this author, on 'contractual practice and dispute settlement in business relations with Arabian states'[19] show, however, that in practice a more pragmatic approach might be taken and exceptions might be admitted in such states. In any case, if a state enterprise falling under such a legal restriction in its home state nevertheless agrees to a choice of law clause in a contract, this clause is not necessarily invalidated by this type of restrictive regulation in its home law. In this respect reference may be made here to the observations made above in section 4.2 on the applicable conflict of laws rules.

18. Böckstiegel, *Der Staat als Vertragspartner ausländischer Privatunternehmen* (Frankfurt 1971).
19. Böckstiegel, *Vertragspraxis und Streiterledigung im Wirtschaftsverkehr mit arabischen Staaten* (Cologne 1981).

4.3.2. Relevance of Mandatory or Public Law Rules of National Law

In arbitrations involving state enterprises, public law rules or other mandatory law rules of the national legal system of the state enterprise may come into consideration more often than in contracts between private enterprises.[20] Such rules will only deal with contracts between private enterprises if there is a specific public interest seen mostly in prohibiting certain contractual practices or restricting certain activities of private enterprises; it is in this context that international arbitrators may have to take into consideration the anti-trust law of a specific state, import, export or transfer restrictions, tax laws and the like. Taking into consideration does not necessarily mean that the contracts and their fulfilment are subject to and regulated by such mandatory rules of a specific state; the consideration may well lead to the result that either the respective state under public international law had no right to rule the respective matter by its national public law or that, in any case, such regulations were not part of the law to be applied to the contract by the parties or the arbitrators. The recent discussions and disputes in connection with the US embargo against the USSR pipeline and the respective contracts of Western European enterprises illustrate the matter, though it cannot be discussed any further here.

Beyond such mandatory or public law rules of general application, rules of specific application to the state, its public entities or its state enterprises in the form of private law companies or corporations may have to be taken into consideration by international arbitrators. Obviously, states may wish to exercise a more extensive or intensive control or influence on the practice of state enterprises to conclude contracts and agree to arbitration clauses in their business relations with foreign enterprises.

The restrictions regarding the submission to arbitration are certainly the most important mandatory type of regulation in this context. They have been already discussed above in section 3.1. Another important mandatory regulation is the restriction on choosing a foreign law as applicable to the contract as is exceptionally found in a case like Saudi Arabia and which has been discussed above in section 4.3.1.

Other mandatory rules of the national law of the state enterprise may bring about restrictions on the state enterprise with regard to the substance of the contract to which private enterprises of that state are not subject. Thus it happens that, in order to promote the interest of the national economy, public entities and other state enterprises have to buy certain goods and services only from national sources, they may be subject to price limits in relation to foreign enterprises or may be allowed only to pay prices in the national currency or only to contract on the basis of certain pre-set conditions of contract. Here again, the existence of such a specific public law or other mandatory rules does not necessarily mean, that they belong to the applicable law and therefore have to be binding for the arbitrators. But obviously their relevance has to be

20. Further details in: Böckstiegel, 'Das anwendbare Recht bei öffentlich-rechtlich geprägten Staatsaufträgen', AWD (1973) 117 ff.; Schlosser, 'Schiedsgerichtsbarkeit und öffentlichrechtliche beeinflußte Streitgegenstände' in *Festschrift Arthur Bülow* (1981), 189 ff.

considered both with regard to their direct influence on the contract and with regard to the practical or legal possibility or impossibility of a party, including the state enterprise, to fulfil certain obligations of the contract. It might be added here that finding one of the parties, including the state enterprise, in a practical or legal impossibility of performing a contractual obligation due to a restriction by such a mandatory rule does not necessarily excuse that party, but may also lead to the result that, since that party was or had to be aware of that impossibility, it may have to pay damages or compensation to the other contractual party.

The information received in this research, especially in respect to question 3.3 confirms first of all that the term 'public law' may have different meanings in different national legal systems, that it has especially little meaning in socialist countries and that even in a classical country for that distinction, France, the specific distinction between public contracts and private law contracts seems to become less relevant. It is for that reason of terminological diversity that public law and mandatory rules of national law are dealt with together here, because what is considered as a rule of public law may simply be considered as a rule of mandatory private law in other states.

From the answers received, the impression is that more often than not no specific public law or mandatory rules of national law can be found with regard to the contracts and arbitrations of state enterprises.

The claim of a state enterprise that it could not or cannot fulfil certain contractual obligations due to such mandatory rules may well need further examination as to the actual existence and applicability of such a mandatory rule, because it is obviously an easy excuse for the enterprise to have at hand. As Barclay (Great Britain) drastically put it: 'Public law is invoked when the state does not wish to pay.'

Other responses seem to take it for granted that public law is predominant (Morocco) or mandatory conditions of contract of the state have to be applied (Code des Marches Publics, France), though in the latter case it does not become quite clear whether this reference only means that in contractual practice contracts will always refer to these conditions for public works.

Public policy is mentioned several times as a limit – but here, of course, the well known discussions of recent years as to the relevance of all aspects of national public policy to international arbitration or to the existence of a more restricted international public policy relevant for international commercial arbitration are at stake and cannot be further gone into here.

4.3.3. Eventual Application of International Law

When the terms 'international law' and 'international contracts' were used in the literature and in arbitration awards or contracts between state entities and foreign private enterprises during the past two decades, the same meaning was not always given to them. In the context of such contracts, as Pierre Lalive[21] rightly points out, 'l'idée apparaît que l'internationalité comporte des degrés',

21. P. Lalive, 'Sur une notion de "Contrat international"', *Multum non Multa, Festschrift für Kurt Lippstein*, (Heidelberg 1980), 135 ff., 138.

thus questioning the traditional limits between the sole alternative national law or public international law. Goldman, in the discussion of the Stockholm Colloquium, stressed the importance of general principles of law in that context, not necessarily, however, the *lex mercatoria*. This is an issue, primarily characterized by the direct participation of the state itself in the contract and the arbitration, and only sometimes, under specific circumstances, involves state enterprises.[22] It is also an issue of such a vast general perspective, leading to discussions on the eventual existence[23] or development of a *lex mercatoria*, transnational law, floating or denationalized arbitrations and the like, that a serious examination is not possible within the scope of this research. I must therefore be permitted here to leave that issue without comment and to deal only with the eventual application of that 'international' law the existence of which is undisputed and which should, for clarification in the above-mentioned discussion, be termed 'public international law'.

Public international law may become relevant to arbitrations with state enterprises in very different ways and that is reflected by the answers received in this research.

First of all the well-known international treaties dealing with commercial arbitration may also be applied if state enterprises are involved in such arbitration. Thus reference has been made in the answers to the European Arbitration Convention of 1961, the Moscow Arbitration Convention for the member states of the Council for Mutual Economic Aid and to the 1965 World Bank Convention on the Settlement of Investment Disputes. With regard to recognition and enforcement, the 1958 New York Convention and other well known instruments dealing with that aspect of international arbitration would have to be added.

Other international treaties applicable may be those concluded in the field of private international law or on the sale of goods. Again there is no reason not to apply them where state enterprises have concluded the contract.

Another aspect of public international law raised in this context is the eventuality of a claim of sovereign immunity. Though the principle of restrictive immunity, accepted more and more generally by courts throughout the world, will already in our context most often lead to the result that immunity cannot be claimed, since the contract has to be considered as being *jure gestiones*, even if the state itself or one of its subdivisions without separate legal personality has concluded the contract, it has been pointed out that nevertheless the claim of sovereign immunity may exceptionally be raised (Argentina, India).

Quite a different sort of application of public international law is at stake if we consider the possibility of that body of law being the proper law of the contract or the applicable substantive law that the arbitrators have to rely on.

As mentioned above, in section 4.3.1, it happens in international contract

22. *Ibid.* p. 135.

23. Only a reference to the most recent decision of the Austrian Supreme Court of November 18, 1982, may be permitted here, since – in dealing with an ICC arbitration award – it seems to be the first court decision accepting, which the arbitrators based their award on, as part of the law. The decision will be published in *Clunet* and RIW.

practice of state enterprises, especially if they are simply subdivisions of the state itself, that a choice of law clause is included in the contract to the effect that public international law should govern the contractual relationship. No information or comments have been received to the effect that such a choice by the parties should not be respected. In fact arbitration practice, especially with regard to investment contracts, shows that arbitrators have accepted such a choice and decided on that basis.

A much more complicated question is whether under specific circumstances it might be necessary to consider public international law as the applicable substantive law even for contracts which do not expressly contain a clause so choosing. The comments received mention that possibility, but also the hesitations in that regard (France, Italy, Korea, Morocco, Nigeria). They also refer to the legal writings and arbitration awards that have come to that result.[24] It is impossible here to consider that most disputed question[25] in much detail. The main problem is of course that public international law is fundamentally made for relations between states and their international organizations because mostly only they are considered as having legal personality in public international law. What is needed therefore, if one wants to extend its application to certain contracts between state entities on one side and private enterprises on the other side, are specific circumstances that may be evaluated to the effect that, at least for the relationship on the basis of that particular contract, the contracting state has accepted the private enterprise as having legal personality under public international law.

In the research work undertaken by me several years ago, mentioned above,[26] on the state as contractual partner of foreign private enterprises, I examined the matter in detail and re-examined it in my main report 'The Legal Rules Applicable in International Commercial Arbitration Involving States or State Controlled Corporations'[27] suggesting the term 'public international law contract'. Therefore, it may suffice to present those criteria which I found to be necessary in order to have a 'public international law contract' and come to the applicability of public international law to such contracts:

(1) On the side of the state partner the contract has to be concluded or authorized by the highest authorities of that state:

(2) the contract must not be of a strictly private law character, but has to contain certain obligations of the state partner either for *ad-hoc* changes of the law or for the execution or non-execution of a specific act of public authority;

(3) the form of conclusion of the contract must be equal or close to that used in that specific state for the conclusion of international treaties;

24. Some recent sources: *Liamco* v. *Libya* arbitration award of 1977, 20ILM (1981) 1 ff.; Rigaux and Weil in *Le Droit des Relations Economiques Internationales, Etudes offertes à Berthold Goldman* (Paris 1982), 261 ff. and 387 ff.

25. Critical: Soruarajah, 'The Myth of International Contract Law', *Journal of World Trade Law* (1981) 187 ff.

26. Böckstiegel, *Der Staat als Vertragspartner ausländischer Privatunernehmen* (Frankfurt 1971), 310 ff.

27. The report will be part of a publication at present being prepared by the ICC on this conference.

(4) the contract must contain a clause excluding national court jurisdiction such as submitting to international arbitration;
(5) it must be evident from the contract either expressly or by implied interpretation that the contract is not supposed to be subject to a national law.

Applying these criteria to contracts of 'state enterprises' as defined for this research leads to the result that only in very exceptional cases can public international law be considered as the applicable law in the absence of an express choice to that effect. This result is in conformity with the respective discussions and resolution of the Institut de Droit International regarding contracts between states and foreign private partners.[28]

5. RELEVANCE OF BEING A SEPARATE LEGAL ENTITY

5.1. The Principle and the Problem

In section 2.2. above, when we discussed the definition of 'state enterprise', it was noted that there is no fixed definition of that term, but that it would be useful in this research to consider as a 'state enterprise' any commercial enterprise predominantly owned or controlled by the state or by state institutions, with or without separate legal personality.

Now, in other sections above it was seen that with regard to certain aspects of arbitration, state enterprises without separate legal personality, which, in other words, are legally part of the state itself, might be subject to specific rules – at least in comparison to those enterprises created as separate legal entities in the form of companies or corporations of private law. It was seen that, for instance, legal restrictions upon submission to arbitration were often only applicable to the state itself or its public entities and that the applicability of national public law or even public international law might be more relevant, or to a certain extent even only possible, with regard to the state itself appearing as contractual partner and party in an arbitration.

These were aspects of a state enterprise in arbitration where indeed it was shown to be relevant whether or not the state enterprise was a separate legal entity from the state or not.

These specific aspects which are important for the involvement of state enterprises in international commercial arbitration are in line with many other legal aspects of the contractual relationship in general (especially liability) where it is also relevant whether or not the state and the state enterprise have separate legal personalities. In principle, if according to the national law of the corporate seat, an enterprise has a separate legal personality, this separation from the owner or owners of the enterprise has to be respected. This also applies to state enterprises, for it is part of the sovereignty of every state to

28. *See* Institut de Droit International, Session d'Athen, *Annuaire 58* (1979) and the Report by Van Hecke, *Les accords entre un Etat et une privée étrangère* (Geneva 1977).

decide that, for certain activities in which the state wishes to engage, it will create an enterprise with separate legal personality and thereby produce the normal legal consequences of such separation. In arbitration also, therefore, in principle and in the great majority of cases, the separation of a state enterprise as a legal entity separate from the state has to be respected.

On the other hand, there have been a number of arbitration cases and many legal discussions and literature dealing with the possibility of and criteria for disregarding the separation between the state and its state enterprise. An issue raised first on the national level and then in international arbitration cases such as *Jordan Investments Ltd.* v. *All-Union Foreign Trade Corporation* of 1958 or the *Rolimpex* cases in the mid-1970s is whether, under certain circumstances, insisting on this separation would not have to be considered as an abuse of the corporate veil or against *bona fide*. This of course is a very fundamental question for state enterprises in their participation in international commerce and also for international commercial arbitration, since this question will have to be considered especially before international arbitral tribunals on the basis of other applicable laws and the specific circumstances of international business relations and not merely under the scope of the respective national law of that state. It is for that reason that this issue was given specific consideration in this research. Since we enter here a disputed and delicate area of the law, it may be useful, on the basis of the information received in this research and in former respective research and practice, to suggest possible criteria only after a more thorough examination of the national and international legal background of, to use some of the terms employed in this context, the 'lifting of the corporate veil', the 'disregard of legal entity' or *Durchgriff*.

5.2. Possibilities of Disregarding the Separation from the State

The phenomenon of state enterprises with a legal personality separate from the state has also had a long tradition in private economy countries. Often states chose that solution trying to get the best of both worlds, an entity 'clothed with the power of government but possessed of the flexibility and initiative of a private enterprise', as President Roosevelt put it when creating the Tennessee Valley Authority in 1933. Other motivations may also play their role, but in fact both at the national level as well as the international level state enterprises play an ever-increasing role.

Each national law, of course, provides its own choices of legal personalities and forms which such state enterprises might take. At the national level, for private corporations as well as for state corporations the question arose, and had to be solved, whether under all circumstances the legal separation from the owner, owners or members of the corporation should be respected. In many developed national legal systems it has then been recognized that under exceptional specific circumstances that separation could not be respected. The doctrine of 'disregard of legal entity' in the United Kingdom and the United

States[29] and of *Durchgriff* in the Federal Republic of Germany[30] and Switzerland[31] are examples of such a lifting of the corporate veil under specific exceptional circumstances in national law. The issue is at present again before the courts and arbitration tribunals in connection with the attempts of foreign creditors to have the legal separation between Iran and its state enterprises disregarded for their claims.[32] Serick's fundamental comparative legal monography[33] as well as comparative studies by Bastid/David[34] and Colm/Simitis[35] on this matter show an astonishing parallelism of jurisdiction and legal theory in many national legal systems.[36]

Though, therefore, the possibility of disregarding the separation between a corporate entity and its owner or members is widely recognized, when considering the problem in the context of arbitration and state enterprises, two basic qualifications make the simple transfer of national law solutions questionable. First of all we are dealing here with international commerce where at least two, if not more, national legal backgrounds, the usages of international commerce and perhaps also international law come in. Secondly, we are dealing with state enterprises and therefore with the question whether specific considerations may have to be taken into account if the state is behind the corporate veil and not private owners or members; a fact which, in particular, US courts seem to take as a reason to lift the corporate veil to an even greater extent.[37] The possibilities developed at the national level of disregarding the legal separation therefore need reconsideration and adaptation in view of several basic differences in our context.

29. For the far-reaching US doctrine *see*: Wormser, Col.L.Rev. 12 (1912) 496 ff.; *US* v. *Milwaukee Refrigerator Transit Co.*, 142 F. 247, 255 (C.C.Wis. 1905); *North Arlington Medical Building Inc.* v. *Sanchez Construction Co.*, 86 Nev. 515, 520, 471 P. 2d 240, 243 (1970). Veltins, 'Durchgriffshaftung im amerikanischen Recht, Piercing the Corporate Veil', RIW (1983) 713 ff. For the UK: *Salmon* v. *Salmon & Co. Ltd.* [1897] A.C. 22; Schmitthoff in Palmer's *Company Law* (1976), para. 18–63 ff. For a comparative view of the US and UK doctrines *see*: Serick, *Rechtsform und Realität juristischer Personen* (Tübingen 1955), 54 ff. and 66, footnotes 1 and 2; Burkhard, *Neuere Probleme des Haftungsdurchgriffs bei juristischen Personen im Recht der Vereinigten Staaten von Amerika*, Diss. (Heidelberg 1969).

30. BGH 3.10.1951 BGHZ 3, 316 ff.; BGH 3.7.1953 BGHZ 10, 205 ff. Böckstiegel, *Der Durchgriff auf den Staat* (Frankfurt 1972), especially 9 ff. Wiedemann, *Gesellschaftsrecht*, Vol. I, 1980, 221 ff.

31. OG Zürich, 19.2.1958, SJZ 1958, 199 f.; BG, 10.5.1950, BGE 76 III 60 ff. Homburger, 'Zum Durchgriff im schweizerischen Gesellschaftsrecht', 67SJZ (1971) 249 ff.

32. Khadjavi-Gontard and Hausmann, 'Haftungsdurchgriff auf ausländische Staaten', *Recht der Internationalen Wirtschaft* (1983) 1 ff.

33. Serick, *Rechtsform und Realität der juristischen Personen* (1955).

34. Bastid/David, *La personalité morale et ses limites* (1960).

35. Colm/Simitis, '"Lifting the Veil" in the Company Laws of the European Continent", 12ICLQ (1963) 189 ff.

36. *See also* Löber (for Austria, Germany and the US), ZfVR (1966), 61 ff. and 145 ff. Hübner (for European countries) JZ (1978) 703 ff.

37. Only a few sources can be cited here: *Banco Nacional de Cuba* v. *First National City Bank of N.Y.*, 270 F.Supp. 1004 (1967), confirmed in so far in 478 F. 2d 191 (1973); *Banca P.C.E. de Cuba* v. *First National City Bank*, 505 F.Supp. 412 (1980); *Electronic Data Systems* v. *Social Security Org. of Iran*, JALR (1980) 848 ff.

- Not one, but several legal systems may have to be considered.
- The relationship between the parties may be subject relatively more to the contract and international trade usages.
- The number and variety of legal forms available are greater internationally than in any specific national system.
- Even a corporate form, which on the face looks the same, may be subject to different legal evaluations due to different national legal, economic and political backgrounds.
- The great variety of choice of law clauses found in connection with arbitration clauses may lead to further qualifications.
- Partners in an international contract are less acquainted with the legal system of the other party and therefore in greater difficulty to provide proof for criteria considered necessary for claims to disregard the legal separation.
- Considerations of public international law or the general principles of law may stop a state from excusing breaches of a contract by claiming that this is due to his own national law.

The answers received to the respective question 5 of our questionnaires on the relevance of being a separate legal entity confirm what is also known in this respect from other sources. Many stress the principle that the separation between the state and the enterprise has to be respected, but many also mention circumstances – more or less exceptional – under which the separation has to be disregarded. Sometimes the answers indicate that perhaps the question was not posed specifically or clearly enough in the questionnaire, because from some countries the principle of respect for the separation is reported without exception though from other sources it is known that courts and legal doctrine have accepted exceptional possibilities of disregarding the separation.

Before general conclusions are drawn and principles or criteria are suggested from the information collected, specific practically important aspects of the relevance of being a separate legal entity have to be considered, namely acts of state as *force majeure* for the state enterprise, the claim of immunity and the consequences of major national interest against fulfilment of a contract.

5.3. Acts of State as Force Majeure for the State Enterprise?

A well-known and highly disputed issue is whether a state enterprise may be excused from non-fulfilment or a breach of contract by claiming *force majeure*, if the state owning or controlling the state enterprise by an act of public authority has interfered. Well-known cases in this context are the USSR ban on oil export leading to the arbitration between *Jordan Investments Ltd.* v. *Sojusneftexport* of 1958[38] and the Polish ban on sugar export leading to the arbitrations between Czarnikow Ltd. and other West European sugar trading houses on one side and Rolimpex on the other side which were finally decided

38. 53 AJIL (1959) 804 ff. See Comments by Domke 24 LCP (1959) 323 f.; Pisar 72 Harv.LR (1959) 1442 with note 98; Berman, 24 RabelsZ (1959) 449 ff.

by the House of Lords in 1978 to the effect that Rolimpex could in fact claim *force majeure* in that case.[39] Similar questions have come up in relation to Iranian state enterprises in the recent past.

From the material received in this research the picture is as varied as it is from the respective international legal discussions.[40] A number of answers to the respective question 5.3 of our questionnaires is to the effect that state enterprises may claim *force majeure* in such cases in the same way as private enterprises. A slightly larger number of answers, however, points out that under specific circumstances the state enterprise may not claim *force majeure* in case of such acts of state. Finally some answers indicate that the problem has not posed itself yet in their national legal system.

In view of the diversity of the answers received and in view of the other material available,[41] conclusions will be suggested below under 5.6 in more general terms as also applicable to the question of *force majeure*. But it should be added here that in many arbitration cases where this issue might be of relevance, the primary and most important source to deal with the problem should be the contract, especially if it defines cases of *force majeure* on one side and the respective responsibilities of the parties on the other side. Sometimes, even if not expressly dealt with in the contract, the general conception and structure of the contract as well as conclusions from specific contractual clauses may permit the definition of 'areas of responsibility' for each of the parties. If impossibility of performing certain contractual obligations is then due to causes within one of these areas of responsibility, the respective party may be held responsible for non-fulfilment or at least for damages even if the respective cause is not due to that party's fault. Commercial contracts very often hold a party responsible without the need to prove fault of that party simply because, in the view of the contractual parties, certain risks are in any case located or placed with one party. Thus, if contractual obligations cannot be fulfilled by a party because its own sub-contractors have not supplied it in time with the necessary materials, no arbitration tribunal would hesitate to hold that party responsible even if it proves that that sub-contractor was carefully chosen and that the non-delivery by that sub-contractor was in no way due to its own fault. Similarly, parties may give express or implied indication in a contract that they consider the granting of certain government licences or the non-issuing of certain governmental prohibitions as falling within the area of responsibility of

39. House of Lords July 6, 1978: [1978] 2 All E.R. 1043m. Court of Appeal May 26, 1955: [1955] 1 All E.R. 81. Comment: Becker, 'The Rolimpex Exit from International Contract Responsibility' 10 *New York University Journal of International Law and Politics* (1978) 447 ff.

40. *See* van Ommenlaghe, 'Les clauses de force majeure et d'imprévision (hardship) dans les contrats internationales', *Revue de droit international et de droit comparé* (1980) 7 ff., 13 ff.; Khadjavi-Gontard/Hausmann, 'Zurechenbarkeit von Hoheitsakten und Subsidiäre Staatshaftung bei Verträgen mit ausländischen Staatsunternehmen', RIW (1980) 533 ff.; Bratons, 'Force majeure en tant que motif de dégagement de la responsabilité dans les contrats de commerce extérieur (pratique de la Commission d'Arbitrage pour le commerce extérieur de Moscou)' in *Arbitrage Commercial, Essais in Memoriam Eugenio Minoli* (Torino 1974), 57 ff.

41. *See also* Gesang, *Force-Majeure* (Königstein 1980), 162 ff. and 175 ff. regarding the socialist states, where this question is also disputed within their internal commercial relations and arbitrations. Further material is also presented and evaluated by von Ommeslaghe, *ibid.* and by Khadjavi-Gontard/Hausmann, *ibid*.

one of the parties simply because that party has the nationality of the respective state and has therefore in any case more means of influencing respective government action or non-action in that particular state. Only if the contract does not permit such an evaluation, the generally suggested principles mentioned below might have to be applied.

5.4. Immunity of the State Enterprise?

Another problem often appearing in practice is the question of whether a state enterprise may claim immunity under certain circumstances.

The material received in this research shows as well as other sources[42] that a general answer to that question is not possible. First of all it may make a difference whether the state enterprise has a separate legal personality from the state or not. Secondly, if it does have separate legal personality, it may make a difference whether it is a public entity or an entity formed as a company or corporation in private law. Thirdly it may make a difference whether the contract and the arbitration only concern commercial activities (*acta jure gestionis*) or whether they also deal with acts of public authority (*acta jure imperii*) as may often be the case in investment disputes.

If the state enterprise does not have a separate legal personality and therefore is legally part of the state itself, the principles developed in court decisions and legal doctrine regarding the immunity of states before courts and arbitral tribunals will have to be applied. This in fact means that, in the majority of countries,[43] the doctrine of restrictive immunity is applicable to the effect that a state may only claim immunity for *acta jure imperii*, acts of public authority, and that a waiver of that immunity may be possible either expressly or by an arbitration clause in a contract also dealing with such acts of public authority. Pieter Sanders, in the discussion of the Stockholm Colloquium, in that context introduced Lord Wilberforce's formula 'Once a trader, always a trader'. Tandeau de Marsac, in the same discussion, pointed out the problems if administrative law is claimed to be part of the applicable law. It seems, however, that, in the majority of international contracts and arbitration disputes with states and state enterprises, such acts of public authority are not at stake, so that the doctrine of restrictive immunity is applicable to the effect that no immunity can be claimed by states for *acta jure gestionis*, commercial activities. It should be added here that immunity is granted in some countries and by some courts to a wider extent or the waiver of immunity is considered not to apply to or be revocable with regard to enforcement and execution of arbitral awards. Then, even where the claim of immunity is not accepted for court proceedings or arbitration proceedings, it may nevertheless be accepted once the judgment or award has to be enforced.

If we now look at those state enterprises that have a separate legal personality from the state, the answers received in this research indicate as well

42. Delaume, 'State Contracts and Transnational Arbitration', 75AJIL (1980) 784, 786 ff.

43. Certain divergencies do appear, however, in the respective discussions of the International Law Commission and in the UN-GA 6th Committee.

as other material[44] that the separation from the state is considered as relevant to the effect that immunity is generally not granted. Of these general comments, only those from Belgium and Nigeria seem to provide for certain reservations. With regard to the Nigerian cement cases, the panel contribution by Ajibola to the Stockholm Colloqiuium available in the Documentation of Material Received[45] gives a survey to the effect that state enterprises, including the Central Bank of Nigeria, were generally not granted immunity. If one includes the comments received specifically to the question whether immunity may be claimed before national courts by such state enterprises, further reservations may be noted from Australia, Brazil, France, Luxembourg and Syria, but only to the effect that under specific circumstances the claim of immunity may not be excluded.

Regarding the possibility of claiming immunity in arbitration proceedings, many answers refer to the eventual restrictions on state enterprises submitting to arbitration as they have been dealt with in section 3.1, above. Obviously, the question of immunity does not arise for all those state enterprises that do not submit to arbitration. On the other hand, the answers either expressly or by implication indicate that, once a state enterprise has legally submitted to arbitration, it cannot claim immunity when the arbitration proceedings actually start.

With regard to specific immunity from execution of arbitral awards, the issue obviously only arises in cases where no immunity has been granted by the courts or by the arbitration tribunal. If immunity is already granted there, no judgment and no award can be reached and the question of execution does not pose itself. Looking therefore only at those cases where no imunity is granted either by state courts or by arbitral tribunals, the information collected indicates that – though normally no immunity will be granted[46] – indeed the claim of immunity may sometimes be accepted once the execution or enforcement against the state enterprise is at stake. At least, comments received from France, Poland and Syria indicate that two different aspects may lead to a limited additional immunity from execution for state enterprises; (1) if the state enterprise is formed as a public entity and not as a private law entity, execution may be limited; (2) or execution may be limited only to certain property, while other property may be considered as immune. The comment from Argentina rightly points out what is confirmed from international contract practice that, in order to have legal security in this context, contractual arbitration clauses may sometimes also include an express waiver of the claim of immunity by the state enterprise for execution.

5.5. Consequences of Major National Interest against Fulfilment of a Contract

We also asked in the questionnaire what would be the consequences, if

44. OLG Frankfurt, 11.5.1981, NJW (1981) 2650 f. and RIW (1981) 484 ff. according to which the National Iranian Oil Company cannot claim immunity against enforcement in Germany.

45. See Chapter VII of this book.

46. OLG Frankfurt, *ibid.*, accepting enforcement against the National Iranian Oil Company.

fulfilment of the contractual duties by the state enterprise should be against a major national interest.

The great majority of answers received points out that in the national law of the contributor the consequences would be the same as if a private enterprise was the party to the contract or the arbitration. This means in effect – as many answers expressly note – that national courts would consider fulfilment of the contract to be limited by public policy, *ordre public*, both in arbitrations with private enterprises and in arbitrations with state enterprises. The question had not been additionally qualified to the effect that arbitrators should also be expected to respect that limit of public policy. Thus, no evaluation is possible in that respect with the scope of this research. Attention should be drawn in this context to the distinction between national public policy and international public policy in the sense of private international law as well as between a 'national' international *ordre public* and an international *ordre public*, properly speaking, which is part of or derives from public international law. In so far as these distinctions have to be taken into account by international arbitrators – sometimes even on the basis of national law such as the new French law for international arbitrations – they are also relevant for arbitration with state enterprises, since the research has not revealed any special treatment in that respect.

Eight answers received from different countries indicate clearly, or seem to indicate, that the conflict with major national interests would have stronger consequences in contracts and arbitrations with state enterprises than with private enterprises. Sometimes it is indicated that the principles of public policy might be applied more extensively if state enterprises are involved. Sometimes it is indicated that this would at least be the case if the contract or the arbitration also applied public law. Sometimes these stronger consequences are indicated without further qualification or explanation.

5.6. Suggested Principles for Lifting the Corporate Veil

When we try to draw conclusions from the general findings and observations mentioned above in sections 5.1 and 5.2, regarding the relevance of the legal separation between a state enterprise and the state itself and regarding specific practically important aspects of that question in sections 5.3, 5.4 and 5.5, above, the primary impression is one of legal insecurity. Not only do answers from different countries come to different results, but sometimes even several answers received from one particular country came to different results regarding certain aspects of the question. Furthermore, as was seen, the criteria for defining those circumstances under which the legal separation between a state enterprise and its state might not be respected, differed very much from country to country and between the concrete legal questions concerned (*force majeure*, immunity, public policy, etc.).

Now, this is not a satisfactory state of affairs for international commerce and international arbitration, because the answer to a usually fundamental question of the contractual relationship, in a claim for contractual performance or damages, is uncertain in the calculation of the parties and in the evaluation of the arbitrators. These uncertainties are increased by additional uncertainties appearing regarding the determination of the applicable law. They are further increased by the great and partially fundamental differences that the various political, economic and legal systems of states throughout the world show regarding the position of state enterprises and the choice of legal forms available to them. It would therefore facilitate international trade and international arbitration considerably if one could come to common denominators, a 'vivre ensemble' (Batiffol),[47] a 'co-existence des systèmes' (Riad).[48] It should especially be worth the effort to try to come to criteria that seem neutral and equally applicable to the socialist and private economy systems of the world. If a state chooses to participate in international commerce by private or state enterprises, that should lead neither to discrimination nor to privileges for the state enterprise. An example of discrimination is that under the Hague Convention of October 18, 1907, and also that of 1923, where state enterprises of neutral states are forbidden to engage in the trading of weapons while private enterprises of neutral states are permitted to do so. As an example of a privilege one may refer to an eventual claim of immunity or to the possibility that the state may help its state enterprise avoid fulfilment of disliked contractual obligations by an appropriate act of public authority. States should not be able to manipulate obligations in international business relations in contracts of their state enterprises. Private enterprises contracting with foreign state enterprises should on the other hand not have additional advantages from the specific character of that contractual partner. This seems to be the basic approach reported and suggested also by Ajibola, Dérains, Craig and Lakhdari on the panel of the Stockholm Colloquium.

On the basis of the material available from this research and other sources,[49] it seems to me that the attempt to try to come to common denominators and criteria should start from what, in our context, the private enterprise and the state enterprise have in common – their function as partners in an international business relationship. This approach, well known from the doctrine of restrictive immunity, takes up the fundamental difference between a state – no matter in what legal form – participating in international commerce on one side and on the other side making use of its sovereign power as a legislator, public administrator or in any other way as a public authority. A functional approach, not dissimilar to Friedmann's 'functional comparison',[50] therefore seems to be best fitted to come to common criteria.

This does not mean that the legal form chosen for the state enterprise is without relevance. If a separate legal entity is created, that is, both for a private person or private enterprise as well as for a state, an expression of a will to produce certain consequences permitted and made available by the respective

47. Batiffol, *Aspects philosophiques du droit international privé*, (Paris 1956), 16.

48. Riad, RdC 108 (1963 I) 625 f. See also the recommendations of the 1st UNCTAD Conference 1964, UN Doc. E/CONF. 46/141 Vol. I, Annex A.I. 3, p. 26.

49. In this context *see* Böckstiegel, *Der Durchgriff auf den Staat* (Frankfurt 1972) with further references as well as the Bibliography and Collection of Cases, Chapter VI.

50. *Legal Theory* (1960), 23.

law of incorporation. The requirements of international business relations discussed lead only to the consequence that this legal separation is not absolutely immune and that the corporate veil may be lifted, if functional considerations make that necessary to avoid discrimination, manipulation or privileges in international trade.[51]

In our context of international arbitration, such common criteria will have to be described in procedural terms, since arbitrators – in the same way as judges – have to decide a case and cannot present a 'draw' to the parties in cases where neither party can prove its point. The method of avoiding such lacunae is of course to work with presumptions to the effect that a specific legal consequence is considered as accepted unless a party proves specific conditions for the opposite consequence. In our context and on the basis of the information available from the answers received and from other sources, the general presumption can only be that the legal separation between the state and the state enterprise, if that state enterprise has been given legal personality of its own, has to be respected. In other words, the state enterprise will be considered to be subject to the same legal rules as private enterprises, unless the specific conditions for those cases are proved and a disregard of the separation and a lifting of the corporate veil is considered possible and necessary.

Starting from a presumption in favour of respecting the legal separation between the state and the state enterprise, therefore, those exceptional cases where the lifting of the corporate veil must be considered possible and necessary will have to be described hereafter.

5.6.1. Estoppel – Actual or Apparent Authority of the State

The principles of estoppel and *venire contra factum proprium* are generally accepted rules both of public international law and of the general principles of law based on the comparison of national legal systems throughout the world. They must be considered applicable if a state enterprise is granted or is allowed to say that it has been granted authority to give certain assurances to the contractual partner on behalf of the state. This is in conformity with Article 7 of the Vienna Convention on the Law of Treaties where it is stated that a person must be considered as validly representing the state if 'it appears from the practice of the States concerned or from other circumstances that their intention was to consider that person as representing the state for such purposes and to dispense with full power'. Similarly the Harvard Law School draft for a convention on the responsibility of states considers the acts of an

51. In his comments to my final report on the Research Project at the 1983 Annual Meeting of the Institute in Paris, Enderlein (GDR) questioned that exceptions could be made and the corporate veil lifted in international relations of state enterprises. This strict approach seems a little astonishing in view of the fact that even in commerce and arbitrations between state enterprises from CMEA countries varying solutions sometimes recognizing, sometimes lifting the corporate veil, have been discussed and practised, and that the GDR especially in bilateral agreements and in its foreign trade arbitration has insisted on lifting the corporate veil and holding state enterprises responsible in cases of certain acts of state. *See*: report by Weidlich in RiA (1974), Heft 3, 9–14, and Gesang, *Force-majeure* (Frankfurt 1980), 167 f., each with many further references. See also note (67) below.

organ of that state as introducing that international responsibility if it acted in 'actual or apparent authority' for that state.[52] In the field of private law, the Federal Court of Justice in the Federal Republic of Germany disregarded the legal separation between a limited company and its sole shareholder if the latter gave the impression to contractual partners that he would fulfil the contracts.[53]

5.6.2. Functional Identity with the State

Furthermore, a state enterprise must be considered as so far identical with the state as it performs acts of public authority, because that is a function exclusively reserved in all countries through the world to the state itself. If therefore the state empowers a state enterprise to perform such functions, it must expect that contractual partners thereby identify that enterprise with the state and therefore consider the legal relationship to that extent as one between the private enterprise and the foreign state. In our context this may become especially relevant with regard to foreign investments, because in investment contracts and development contracts between states and foreign investors we often find clauses dealing with such aspects of public authority as taxation, expropriation, exploitation licences and concessions, transfer authorizations, police requirements, etc. If contracts dealing with such matters are concluded by state enterprises with the permission of the state, then the invalidity of such clauses may not be claimed later on the basis of the legal separation between the state enterprise and the state. Whether a specific function is to be considered as one of public authority will normally have to be decided on the basis of the law of the state and state enterprise. Thus, the Cour de Cassation in France refused to accept a claim against the Banque d'Espagne, since in that case the bank had issued an 'Acte de la Puissance publique'.[54] While in that case the functional identity led to an advantage for the state enterprise, it led to a disadvantage when a court in New York rejected a claim of the Banco do Brazil because that concrete claim against a private person living in New York was considered as an enforcement of Brazilian public rules on foreign currency on the territory of the United States.[55] In Germany *Sphärenvermischung*[56] and functions of public authority[57] have been accepted as criteria for disregarding the legal separation. When in 1965 enforcement of an arbitration award was sought in the well known *Sapphire* case against the National Iranian Oil Company, the District Court of The Hague disregarded the legal separation between NIOC and the Iranian state, because NIOC had granted the concession in the respective concession contract and had in doing so performed a function *jure imperii* so that it could claim immunity in view of the court.[58]

52. 55 AJIL (1961) 576.
53. *Volkswagen Savers Case*, BGH 9.12.1958 (Akt. 7 VIII ZR 80/56), p. 49 of the judgment.
54. *Epoux Martin* c. *Banque d'Espagne*, Rev.Crit. DIP (1953) 425.
55. *Banco do Brazil, S.A.* v. *A.C. Israel Commodity Co.*, 12 N.Y. 2d 371, 239 N.Y.S. 2d 872 (1963) 924 f.
56. Wiedemann, *Gesellschaftsrecht I* (1980), 224.
57. Böckstiegel, *Der Durchgriff auf den Staat*, (Frankfurt 1972), 20 ff.
58. 5 ILM (1966) 477 ff. Arbitration Award of March 15, 1963, 13 ICLQ (1964) 1011 ff.

Though this is another example of functional identity as far as granting the concession is concerned, the result arrived at by the court does not seem convincing because the concession was only one aspect of the contract while many other aspects were *lege gestionis* and secondly the submission to arbitration must be considered as a waiver of immunity.

5.6.3. Evasion of Obligations – Abuse of Rights

It is a generally accepted principle in both national and international law, already recognized by the Permanent Court of International Justice, that a state may not abuse legal forms and rights to evade obligation (*abus de droit, Rechtsmißbrauch*).[59] This principle has also been applied in national laws with the effect that the corporate veil was lifted.[60] It may in appropriate cases be applied by international arbitrators. Whether it is applicable will, as before national courts, always depend on the specific circumstances of the arbitration case. Though the principle of applicability is beyond doubt, it seems difficult to describe appropriate cases in the abstract.

There is, however, a further and more specific application of that principle which may also be considered in international arbitration with state enterprises.

When a state makes use of its powers of control and legislation to change the legal form of a state enterprise in order to evade the obligations of that state enterprise in a contract and an arbitration clause, this must be considered an abuse of rights. An example is the case *Société des Grands Travaux de Marseille* v. *(East Pakistan Industrial Development Corporation), Bangladesh Industrial Development Corporation and the Republic of Bangladesh*. Therefore, the arbitration award of May 31, 1973,[61] holding the defendants severally liable seems convincing, while the decision of the Swiss Federal Tribunal of May 5, 1976,[62] with a contrary result is most objectionable, as has been pointed out by Pierre Lalive.[63]

It is only in international arbitrations in which public international law is the applicable law, or at least part of the applicable law, that the corporate veil between the state enterprise and the state itslef may have to be lifted if a state has tried to evade its own obligations in public international law by letting one of its state enterprises perform functions which for the state itself would be a breach of public international law. This is a consequence of the well-known principle that a state may not excuse itself for breaches of obligations in public international law by reference to its own national law and therefore also not by

59. Of the many sources one may refer to: PCIJ 1930, Series A, No. 24, 12 and No. 46, 167; PCIJ 1926, Series A, No. 7, 30. Oppenheim-Lauterpacht, 1 §155, aa; Rousseau, *Principes Généraux du Droit International Public*, 904.

60. Examples from US law: *Wull* v. *Colt Co.*, 31 F.R.D. 154 (F.D.N.Y. 1962); *Walkovsky* v. *Carlton*, 223 N.E. 2d 6 (1966). Examples from German Law: BGH, WM 1958, 463; BGH, WM 1960, 1119. Specially for obligations of the State: Böckstiegel, *Der Durchgriff auf den Staat* (Frankfurt 1972), 23 ff.

61. Partly reprinted in *Yearbook Commercial Arbitration*, Vol. V (1980), 179 ff.

62. 102 ATF Ia 574, *Yearbook Commercial Arbitration*, Vol. V (1980), 217 ff.

63. 34 *Annuaire Suisse de Droit International* (1978) 387 ff., 400 and in more detail in 97 *Revue de Droit Suisse* (1978) 529 ff. (Arbitrage international et ordre public suisse).

reference to legal forms for state enterprises available in its own national law. An example is cited by Seidl-Hohenveldern[64]: a state that has accepted an obligation in public international law to open an airport to foreign aircraft without discrimination may not fix excessive landing fees, even if they also apply to his own national airline, because the legal separation between that national airline and the state has to be disregarded, since the fees paid by that national airline are again income for the respective state and therefore an economic burden is placed only on foreign aircraft. Similar situations may arise in international arbitration in connection with those many investment protection treaties concluded between western industrialized states and third world states and also in connection with contracts concluded between states and foreign private investors if those states fulfil the requirements mentioned above in section 4.3.3 for the applicability of public international law.

5.6.4. Responsibility for Acts of Public Authority

Finally, coming to the disputed question of whether and under what circumstances state enterprises may excuse non-fulfilment of contractual obligations by claiming *force majeure* due to acts of public authority by their own state, here also the starting point will have to be the principle that the separation between the state enterprise and the state is respected and that therefore normally acts of public authority by the state have to be accepted as an excusing case of *force majeure*.

On the other hand, it should be realized that the question of *force majeure* does not arise in all cases of state interference. If the contract itself stipulates that the state enterprise is to be considered responsible for certain acts of state, no *force majeure* can be claimed if such an act of state then actually occurs. The same applies, if the applicable national law – as some do[65] – expressly holds the exporting party responsible for getting the required export licence. The INCOTERMS of the the International Chamber of Commerce also provide for such a responsibility, and therefore in cases where the contract contains a reference to FOB-delivery, again the seller cannot claim *force majeure*.[66] In addition, an act of state cannot be considered as *force majeure* if it is proved that a party has formally applied or informally asked for the act; and often a party may be held responsible for an act of state because available remedies against the act were not exhausted. As mentioned above under section 5.3, interpretation of the contract may also lead to certain 'areas of responsibility' with the effect that causes within such areas will lead to liability, even if the party was not negligent or at fault in any way. In all such cases, a party may not claim *force majeure* regardless of whether it is a private enterprise or a state enterprise. Only in cases when no such specific provisions or considerations are applicable,

64. ROW (1966) 6 f.

65. Called a 'usual role' for US law in *Banking and Trading Corp. Ltd.* v. *Reconstruction Finance Corp.*, 147 F.Supp. 193 (1956) 208 f. For the UK *see Peter Cassidy Seed Ltd.* v. *Osuustrukakaupa J.L.* [1957] 1 All E.R. 484, 487, 489.

66. ICC, *Incoterms* (1980 edition) FOB, A.3. See also the *Commentary to the Incoterms* by Eisemann/Melis (Vienna 1980) 102 ff.

does the general question arise of which rule should apply in view of the fact that it is after all a state enterprise claiming *force majeure* due to the act of some other organ of that same state.

Here also the basic approach must be that the state enterprise must be neither privileged nor discriminated against in comparison with the private enterprise. Thus, the mere fact that a socialist state decides to exercise a state monopoly on foreign trade does not justify the conclusion that all acts of state are attributed to it as a contractual partner and therefore no act of state could be considered as an excused case of *force majeure*. On the other hand, not every act of state can be recognized as a *force majeure* just because a different organ of the state issues the act, for, in centrally planned economies and state trading countries the state could then always 'provide a *force majeure*' if the fulfilment of the contract is no longer considered advantageous. Therefore, even in commerce and arbitrations between the socialist countries, varying solutions, sometimes recognizing, sometimes refusing, *force majeure* for state enterprises have been disputed and practised.[67] Finally, this again is to a certain extent also an application of the abuse of rights principle mentioned above.

In view of the above-mentioned consideration that, for an arbitration tribunal, the question will mostly pose itself as a matter of proof and presumption, and taking further into account that the state party is in a much better position to provide details of proof on the background of its own acts of state, the following rules[68] could be applied:

A. *Acts of state in the form of administrative acts*

1. Due to the presumption that a state will not have its executive organs act to the detriment of its own foreign trade organs, including state enterprises, administrative acts of state should in principle not be considered as *force majeure*.
2. This presumption is not applied, however, if it can be seen *prima facie* or can be proved by the state enterprise that the administrative act was caused by general considerations not connected with this contract or this sort of contract.
3. In spite of rule A2 the presumption under A1 is applicable again, if the private party proves that in its specific case the general considerations did not apply.

67. *Force majeure* has been recognized by Bulgarian and Polish arbitration, refused by the arbitration of Hungary and the German Democratic Republic. As was communicated by Stalev in a comment of October 1983, this old practice of Bulgarian arbitration has since changed and now acts of economic planning are no longer recognized as *force majeure* for state enterprises. On the other hand see also the recent doubts by Enderlein mentioned above in note 51. The issue has also been discussed in the meetings of the presidents of the foreign trade arbitration institutions of the CMEA states and neither view fully prevailed. For further details and sources *see* Gesang, *Force-majeure* (Königstein 1980), 167 f. For the USSR *see* Bratons in *Arbitrage Commercial, Essais in Memoriam Eugenio Minoli* (Torino 1974), 57 ff.

68. Principles which go further have been suggested by Khadjavi-Gontard/Hausmann, RIW (1980) 533 ff. and RIW (1983) 1 ff. and exemplified by application to Iranian state enterprises.

B. Acts of state in the form of law

1. If it is not a general law but a law for an individual case, the same rules apply as under A.

2. A general law, due to its *per definitionem* general character, will in principle have to be recognized as *force majeure*.

3. Rule B2 does not apply, however, if the private enterprise supplies at least *prima facie* evidence that it was in the interest of the state not to fulfil its contractual obligations which was the motivation of the law.

It should be noted that these rules, which were suggested by this author on an earlier occasion, have been accepted in a large international arbitration in Switzerland by a decision of September 9, 1983, in which the arbitral tribunal evaluated a claim of *force majeure* by an Eastern European state enterprise on the basis of these rules.[69] It might also be of interest that these rules, when they were presented by the author in his main report on 'The Legal Rules Applicable in International Commercial Arbitration Involving States and State Controlled Corporations' to the 1983 Paris conference for the 60th anniversary of the ICC Court of Arbitration, found wide support from participants including Jimenez de Arechaga, former President of the International Court of Justice.[70]

In practical examples the rules mean: if in a state-trading country the state refuses an export or import licence, this is not normally a case of *force majeure* (A1). If the state party proves that general political considerations such as a food shortage for its population or a war in the designated delivery country has led to the refusal of the export licence, this is accepted as *force majeure* (rule A2). If a foreign investor does not receive the transfer of profits due from a state enterprise because the transfer law has been changed by the legislative body, this is a case of *force majeure* (rule B2). If, however, he applies evidence that the law was directed to stop payments to the foreign investors and keep the funds for other purposes of the respective state enterprises, the law is not accepted as a case of *force majeure* (rule B3).

It is not seriously suggested that the criteria mentioned above would solve every problem in relation to claims of *force majeure* by state enterprises or that the undisputed acceptance of these criteria can be expected by all private enterprises, state enterprises and arbitrators having to deal with that question. But it is suggested that these general presumptions, on the basis of practical cases and legal literature in this field, could be of assistance in dealing with this issue in a way which can be calculated in advance and which takes into account the reasonable interests, procedural possibilities and access to eventual evidence of both sides concerned.

69. The award is not yet published.

70. The proceedings of the conference are at present being prepared for publication by the ICC.

6. ENFORCEMENT OF ARBITRATION AWARDS AGAINST STATE ENTERPRISES

6.1. Need for Enforcement in Practice?

One often notices a tendency in discussion of international arbitration to overestimate the question of enforcement. This may be partly due to the New York Convention as the major international instrument on arbitration. This may be also due to the general fact that lawyers tend to discuss rather the pathological cases than the cases that proceed without problems. Every research into the practice of international arbitration shows that by far the great majority of arbitration awards is fulfilled without the need for enforcement. On the other hand, of course, it may be said that this is so only because the losing parties know that otherwise the award could be enforced, especially due to the New York Convention. Thus, no doubt, the possibility of enforcement has an indirect influence on the voluntary fulfilment of arbitration awards. In addition, Terki, from the Algerian perspective, rightly pointed out in the discussion at the Stockholm Colloquium that even an unenforceable award may be the basis of claims on state insurance or guarantee arrangements.

This general picture in international arbitration is also confirmed by the information collected with regard to state enterprises involved in international commercial arbitration. The vast majority of answers received indicates that state enterprises will in practice fulfil arbitration awards voluntarily so that enforcement does not become necessary.

There are also, however, some indications that state enterprises, be they of a legal personality separate from the state or not, may be more difficult in fulfilling arbitration awards. If it is mentioned several times that state enterprises at least have been found to be slower in fulfilling awards, that may be the result either of the more complicated and slower decision-making procedures existing within a state enterprise or because the state enterprise may have to apply for authorization from the state itself. Though not indicated in the answers to our questionnaires, practical experience in recent years also shows that sometimes a state enterprise may try to avoid or at least delay fulfilment of an award simply because it cannot receive the necessary funds, especially in hard currency, from its own or the state's resources for fulfilment – a situation not uncommon today when many states find it difficult or even impossible to fulfil payment obligations they have entered into with foreign creditors.

6.2. Eventual Specific Requirements for Enforcement

If and when enforcement of an arbitration award against a state enterprise becomes necessary, first of all the requirements which generally have to be fulfilled for all arbitration awards have to be met. This means in fact that national arbitration awards can be enforced by the procedure laid down in the respective national law which is also applicable to enforcement against state enterprises. For the enforcement of foreign arbitration awards, in addition to the procedure laid down in the respective national law of the state of enforcement, international conventions to which that state is a party may have to be taken into account, especially the New York Convention of 1958. All these requirements for enforcement of arbitration awards are also applicable for enforcement against state enterprises.

When we turn to the question of whether additional specific requirements of enforcement[71] may have to be fulfilled if enforcement of the arbitration award is directed against a state enterprise, a distinction becomes necessary between enforcement in a foreign state on the one hand and enforcement in the home state of the state enterprise on the other hand.

Enforcement against the state enterprise outside the territory of its home state may sometimes be attacked by the state enterprise claiming immunity. The information received in answer to questions 5.3 and 5.3.3 of the questionnaires and from other sources, as summarized above in section 5.4, shows that in some states courts may accept a claim of immunity against enforcement or execution even if such a claim would not be accepted against court proceedings or arbitration proceedings. This may sometimes be due to the judgment that enforcement is a more intensive interference with the rights of the foreign state or that submission to arbitration may only be interpreted as a waive of immunity with regard to the arbitration proceedings, but not necessarily with regard to the enforcement of the award. Sometimes the doctrine of restrictive immunity will lead to the effect that enforcement of the arbitration award will only be allowed against those property rights of the state enterprise or the state (if the state enterprise does not have a separate legal personality) that belong to the commercial activities of the state enterprise, but not against property rights of the state that belong to public functions or sovereign activities of the state. Thus, where the state enterprise does not have a legal personality of its own and therefore the state itself is legally the losing defendant in the arbitration award, enforcement may be permitted against shares which the state may have in a foreign company, but not on houses, furniture or equipment used for embassies or consulates. It may be noted in this context that even in the 1965 Convention on the Settlement of Investment Disputes, in which recognition and enforcement of the arbitration awards has been facilitated, Article 55 provides that these facilities shall not 'be construed as derogating from the law in force in any Contracting State relating to immunity of that state or of any foreign state from execution'.

If we now turn to the enforcement of arbitration awards against state enterprises in their home states, the information collected shows many variations between national laws. Though it is generally indicated that enforcement against the state enterprise is possible in principle, in many countries specific requirements or limitations have to be respected, many of them similar or equal to those limitations and requirements that also apply for the enforcement of judgments of state courts against state enterprises.

In many countries enforcement is not possible in so far as it would interfere

71. *See also* Delaume, *ibid*., 75 AJIL (1981) 809 ff.

with the fulfilment of public functions by the state or its entities. Sometimes this limit is set by the national law in a functional approach so that it applies to any property rights used for public functions no matter whether the state enterprise has no separate legal personality, or has a separate legal personality in the form of a public entity or in the form of a company or corporation of private law. Sometimes a juridical approach is taken by the national laws in such a way that enforcement is restricted with regard to state enterprises having the legal form of public entities, while it is not restricted with regard to those in the form of companies or corporations of private law. Sometimes both approaches appear in a certain mixture such as in § 882a of the German Code of Civil Procedure.

In a number of countries enforcement against state enterprises is only possible by specific procedures. Either special authorizations from the state or its courts may be necessary (examples: Australia and Morocco); sometimes certain grace periods have to be respected before enforcement can take place (examples: Federal Republic of Germany and India).

Again, in certain countries, enforcement may only be possible against certain property rights or certain bank accounts (examples: Bulgaria and Poland).

The general conclusion therefore is that, even if the general conditions for fulfilment, such as those of the New York Convention, are fulfilled, enforcement of arbitration awards against state enterprises, though normally possible, may be subject to specific requirements both in the home state of the state enterprise and in other states.

7. SUGGESTIONS FOR IMPROVEMENT

7.1. Improvements in Contract Practice

There is one improvement in contract practice[72] which is by far the most often mentioned in the comments received. Arbitration clauses in contracts with state enterprises should be phrased much more carefully and more clearly. This is especially mentioned with regard to some of the specific issues arising with involvement of state enterprises in arbitration as they have been dealt with above.

The second most mentioned suggestion for improvement is to the effect that, either in the arbitration clause or in another contractual clause, the parties should specify the law applicable to their contract.

Some comments have again pointed out in this context the usefulness of arbitration and therefore stressed that at least in their contracts with foreign partners state enterprises should submit to arbitration.

Eisemann, in the discussion at the Stockholm Colloquium pointed out that it can be useful, and for arbitrations in specific countries even absolutely necessary, to include a contractual provision on the procedure of the arbitration with regard to enforceability.

72. In that context see also Kopelmanas, 'La procédure arbitrale dans les contrats internationaux de travaux publics' in *Arbitrage Commercial, Essais in Memoriam Eugenio Minoli* (Torino 1974), 273 ff.

Other comments have suggested the following improvements: more information should be supplied on state enterprises; the persons authorized by state enterprises should be clearly defined; if the national law of the state enterprise is the law applicable to the contract, it should be made clear that this means the state of the law at the time of the conclusion of the contract so that later changes in that national law should be disregarded by the parties in performing the contract and by international arbitrators in deciding a dispute (freezing the applicable law).

7.2. Suggestions for Arbitration Practice

With regard to arbitration practice, a number of suggestions have been put forward without one particular suggestion drawing considerably more comments than the others.

Several comments stress that arbitration procedures with state enterprises need to be speeded up because most of the time they tend to be slower than normal arbitration.

Sanders and Haug, in the discussion of the Stockholm Colloquium, stressed the need for the selection of highly qualified arbitrators. Several comments were also received to the effect that, specifically, persons active in state administrations or state enterprises often lack sufficient information on international commercial arbitration so that educational efforts in this direction might be useful. In that context special reference was made to the need of such efforts in developing countries. On the other hand, Lakhdari, in his contribution on the panel of the Stockholm Colloquium, suggested that more presidents of arbitration tribunals should be chosen from third world countries. Another communication received in the research pointed out also that presidents of arbitration tribunals are seldom chosen from the United States or a seat in the United States is rarely chosen, since US enterprises are so often parties to arbitrations that a 'third' country has to be selected.

Other comments suggested the following: the procedure of arbitration should be more clearly defined; more room should be given to the possibility of conciliation; more attention should be granted to the necessity of independence of the arbitrators nominated by state enterprises; arbitration awards should be published more often; a prior exchange of statements on the evidence to be submitted by both parties would most often be useful and speed up the procedure.

Absolutely equal treatment should be granted to the state enterprise and the private enterprise. When useful and possible, third parties which might be facing regress claims should be included in the arbitration procedure right from the beginning – a possibility frequently discussed in recent years under the topic of multi-party arbitration. If one of the parties, including the state enterprise, is not co-operating in the arbitration, a firm position should be taken by the arbitrators.

Finally, a necessary and certainly realistic attitude is reflected in the comment from Boris Ryvkine (France) when he simply asks for patience in arbitrations with state enterprises.

7.3. Suggestions for Changes in National Law

Of the changes suggested for national law, several of those most often mentioned lead in the same direction:

State enterprises should generally be authorized to submit to arbitration in the same way as private enterprises. Special arbitration rules for state enterprises should be deleted in national law. National laws should lead to promotion of arbitration, and this should also be the case for the international commercial contracts of state enterprises.

Some comments stress that the possibility of interference by state courts in arbitration or in the control of arbitration awards should be reduced, especially in common law countries where the 'case stated' procedure still exists.

Some comments speak in favour of deleting or at least reducing the possibility of claiming immunity.

With regard to enforcement, one group of comments speaks in favour of deleting any privileges for state enterprises in the enforcement of awards, while another group of comments speaks in favour of a wider ratification of the international arbitration conventions, especially the New York Convention of 1958.

Finally, reference should be made here to the present work of UNCITRAL on a model arbitration law. If that model is established, states that now do not offer an effective basis for arbitration may more easily come to an effective adaptation of their national laws. But that is a long way off.

7.4. Suggestions for Changes in International Law

With regard to eventual improvements in international law, the suggestion most often mentioned is that the claim of immunity should be eliminated for state enterprises. This suggestion is partly mentioned as a recommended change of general international law, partly as a recommendation to include special clauses in international treaties to that effect. In the same context it is also suggested that clauses should be included in treaties to the effect that state enterprises and states themselves may submit to arbitration. Partly in relation to the suggestions to eliminate immunity is the suggestion received that all privileges of state enterprises with regard to the enforcement of arbitration awards should be eliminated.

Other comments suggest that, in international arbitration and the respective treaties and rules, more consideration should be given to the developing countries. One example mentioned of how that could be done is that the seat of the arbitration tribunal should more often be in developing countries.

Several comments suggest that it would be useful to develop more rules of substantive international law on international commerce and international commercial arbitration. In that context it is also suggested that state enterprises should be recognized as international persons. It does not become clear whether this is supposed to include state enterprises in the form of companies or corporations of private law, and, in the affirmative, whether then also the international legal personality of private enterprises is suggested, as has been proposed in a number of publications and arbitration awards where the applicability of public international law was at stake.

Jean Robert, in the discussion at the Stockholm Colloquium, presented the view that a renegotiation of the New York Convention might be necessary, especially in view of the greater involvement of third world countries in international arbitrations. As is known from other discussions, many feel, on the other hand, that this is neither necessary or opportune.

Finally, one comment in this context also rightly draws attention to the present activities of UNCITRAL in trying to draft a model law on arbitration. Indeed, some of the difficult problems mentioned above might well be reduced in the future if clear provisions could be agreed upon in that model law and if, in addition, that model law would in the long run be accepted in many states, irrespective of whether this is by way of an international convention or merely by way of a recommendation for inclusion into national law.

8. CONCLUDING COMMENTS

The reader may not be surprised if the general rapporteur at the end of this research describes his attitude towards the results as ambivalent.

On one side the information collected through the questionnaires and by other means can certainly be considered to be most useful. It can certainly contribute to achieving a better basis for the state of arbitration practice, of national law and of legal opinion throughout the world with regard to a topic of practical and theoretical importance. Even if users of this publication may not always agree with the comments reproduced from the answers received or given by the general rapporteur in conclusion, they may still be in a better position to come to their own conclusions on the respective questions.

On the other hand I do not feel completely satisfied with the results of this research. To a certain extent, of course, this is always the case in legal research, because there will always remain certain points on which one would wish that more information had been available or more details had been discussed. In an international research effort as undertaken here, where one is more dependent than normally on secondary information regarding the state of a national law and the state of arbitration practice, further shortcomings are unavoidable. This is especially so if the research is dealing with a topic which – as do others in international commercial arbitration – has many aspects of a confidential character. Many accidental circumstances will then influence the volume and the kind of information becoming available. It is often the case that those best informed have the least time to supply detailed information. But it should be added here that – as a glance at the list of contributors confirms – a great number of the most prominent personalities and institutions in this field have taken the time to supply information. This as well as the large attendance of distinguished experts in international arbitration at the Stockholm colloquium indicate that the topic 'Arbitration and State Enterprises' is widely considered as one of both practical and theoretical legal importance.

If this volume presents only the summary and conclusions of the general rapporteur, this is due to the enormous quantity of information and material received which made reproduction in this volume impossible, mainly for financial reasons. If nevertheless, as presented in Chapter VII of this book, a Documentation of Material Received is made available as authentically as possible, this is in tribute on the one hand to the many experts throughout the world who have taken the time to co-operate in this effort and, on the other hand, in tribute to the reader who, in my view, should be given an opportunity to make his own evaluation from the material received in answer to the questionnaires.

If this publication and research project is able to produce more than a normal monograph by a single person could do, this is due to the most generous co-operation of experts throughout the world. To them we owe gratitude as well as to the members of the Academic Council and the Corresponding Members of the Institute of International Business Law and Practice who have also contributed their comments and advice. In this context, I feel I should specially mention how grateful I am to my colleague Pierre Lalive who, as president of the Institute and an expert in the matter, has contributed from his wisdom. Special mention should also be made of Xavier Giocanti, Administrative Director of the Institute, who has been extremely helpful in many technical matters which obviously are most important in international research of this kind. The collection of information world-wide would not have been possible without the financial assistance and the facilities of the staff at the headquarters in Paris and in the national branches of the International Chamber of Commerce. A very valuable financial contribution was also received from the Verein der Freunde und Förderer der Universität Köln (Society of the Friends and Supporters of Cologne University). Finally, I owe a personal word of thanks to my team at the Chair of International Business Law at the University of Cologne where especially Ms. Maiwald, Dr. Catranis, Ms. Wolff, Ms. Schmaus, Mr. Boris, Mr. Frantzen, Mr. Georgieff and Mr. Lenz have been most helpful in supervising the collection of information and the production of the manuscript for this publication and the Documentation of Material Received.

KARL-HEINZ BÖCKSTIEGEL

CHAPTER IV

PROCEDURE OF THE RESEARCH

A. METHOD

Though methodological considerations are sometimes overestimated in modern research, at least in some countries and in some fields of the law, there can be no doubt about the relevance of the method applied in an international research of the kind that we have here. Especially in the field of international business law and practice we find great differences in evaluation and results due to differences in the methods applied by the respective authors, arbitrators or judges. The scale runs from the purely academic reflection of an author sitting somewhere in a secluded ivory tower and granting the reader the benefit of his thinking on the basis of a limited quantity and quality of material which he happens to have available, all the way to the purely pragmatic presentation either factually of a particular business practice or legally of what the law should be in the interest of a client of a particular lawyer.

The choice of a research method is obviously very much dependent on what one tries to achieve by the research. This is also the case here. The aim was not to add yet another publication to those on state enterprises or those on international commercial arbitration. The aim was to collect a basket of information not available in any other publication both on the practice and the law of the involvement of state enterprises in international commercial arbitration by making use of the unequalled possibilities of access presented by the Institute of International Business Law and Practice on one side to most eminent international lawyers and on the other side to the international business community and the experience available there.

In view of this approach the role of the General Rapporteur had to be defined: though obviously he was responsible for the procedure of the research project, the contents of the questions asked and the criteria given for the collection of information, he had to ensure that the information collected remained as authentic as possible and was not later on communicated only through the filter of his own evaluation. Though he had probably been asked to direct this research project in view of his former publications and practical experience in this field, he had to resist the temptation to look only for confirmation of his views expressed earlier. The publication of this report on the research project, therefore, tries as much as possible to present the information collected. Since the enormous quantity of the information and documents received made reproduction in this volume impossible, mainly for financial reasons, for those having a special interest the Documentation of Material Received is made available as presented in Chapter VII of this book.

Though it was obviously necessary to exclude from that Documentation some information and material submitted which had no or only vague relevance to the topic, the information and material included normally remains unchanged. Thus, the reader can make his or her own evaluation of the information and does not have to accept the evaluation of the Rapporteur.

The chronology of the research project may be summarized shortly as follows: early in 1980 I was aproached by the Institute with the question whether I would be prepared to direct this research as General Rapporteur. I agreed and presented a tentative draft of procedure which was accepted by the Academic Council. The two questionnaires were worked out as presented in sections C and D below – Questionnaire I to collect information on national law and practice and Questionnaire II to collect information on arbitration practice. These questionnaires, in 1980 and 1981, were then widely distributed to the business community, arbitrators and universities throughout the world. The answers, reactions and documents received obviously vary widely both in their volume and in the kind of information supplied. In October 1981, the Annual Meeting of the Institute of International Business Law and Practice was combined with the Stockholm Symposium on this research project as presented in Chapter V of this book. Further information was received thereafter and a final report by the General Rapporteur was presented to and discussed by the September 1983 Annual Meeting of the Institute in Paris.

B. STATISTICS

Statistical Data I

I. Total number of contributions received: 92

II. Total number of countries and international institutions involved: 40

III. The contributions received cover the following countries and international institutions:

Argentina:	1	Hong Kong:	1
Australia:	1	India:	1
Austria:	2	Ireland:	1
Belgium:	6	Indonesia:	1
Brazil:	2	Italy:	7
Bulgaria:	1	Korea (Rep.):	1
Canada:	1	Luxembourg:	3
Chile:	1	Mexico:	1
Colombia:	1	Morocco:	2
Czechoslovakia:	1	Netherlands:	2
Denmark:	1	Nigeria:	1
Finland:	2	Poland:	2
France:	10	Saudi Arabia:	2
Germany (Fed. Rep):	8	Sweden:	2
Germany (Dem. Rep.):	1	Switzerland:	8
Great Britain:	6	Syria:	2

Turkey:	2	IATA:	1
Uganda:	1	ICC:	1
USA:	1	ICSID:	2
Yugoslavia:	1	NATO:	1

Statistical Data II* A Sample of Recent Awards of ICC Arbitrations in which States or State Enterprises are Involved

I. Period studied: January 1979 to July 1980

II. Number of cases: approx. 380

III. Disputes involving a state or state enterprise: 113 (29.7%)

IV. Disputes in which state or state enterprises are claimants: 38/113

V. Countries involved

- Africa
- Middle East
- Eastern Europe
- India
- Latin America

VI. Fields of activity

- Supplying of equipment
- Engineering
- Civil engineering and construction

VII. Causes of disputes

- Delay in execution of contractual obligation
- Bad-functioning
- Modification of the buyer's conditions

In most cases, the disputes involve technical questions rather than legal points.

C. QUESTIONNAIRE I. NATIONAL LAW AND PRACTICE

1. Dear Reader,

I am quite aware that answering this questionnaire means additional work for you. Nevertheless I would be grateful if you could give us your answers as best as you can, because this is still the easiest way both for you and for us to collect valuable information for an important research, and because otherwise

* Data collected by Mr. Xavier Leducq, France.

– your own expertise and views would not be included in the research,
– your country or institution would not be included in the final report or might be represented by information and views from other sources which are less correct or precise.

Thank you very much in advance.

Prof. Dr. Karl-Heinz Böckstiegel
General Rapporteur for the Research Project

2. *Explanation of the term 'State Enterprise'.* In this questionnaire, 'state enterprise' is understood to be any commercial enterprise predominantly owned or controlled by the state or by state institutions, with or without separate legal personality.

3. *Your way to answer the questions.* If not indicated otherwise, answers should be given on the basis of your national law and practice.

If you wish to explain or qualify any of your answers, you may do so either in the space left after each question or on a separate sheet with reference to the number of the question.

4. Though answering every question will help us to take full account of your specific expertise and background in the final report, we would still be grateful to receive your answers, if you can only answer certain questions.

5. Name and address of institution and/or person that has answered this questionnaire should be given in full detail:
Name:
Address:
Phone:
Date:

6. Please return the questionnaire as soon as possible to
Prof. Dr. Karl-Heinz Böckstiegel
Chair of International Business Law
Universität zu Köln
Albertus-Magnus-Platz
D-5000 Köln 41

Question 1 (Survey of arbitration practice of state enterprises)

Q.1.1. Do state enterprises in your country in their commercial contracts agree to arbitration?

generally
often
seldom
never
only in their international contracts

Q.1.2. To what sort of arbitration will they normally agree?

International Chamber of Commerce
UNCITRAL
ICSID
Ad hoc-Arbitration
Which national institution?
Which other?

Q.1.3. Which legal restrictions exist, if any, for state enterprises agreeing to arbitration? Please add text and English translation or summary.

Q.1.4. Could you provide us with reports on/or texts of any arbitration awards involving state enterprises? Please enclose (if not in English, additional English summaries would be helpful):

I enclose texts of such awards.
I enclose reports on such awards.
I enclose references where such awards have been published.

Question 2 (Survey of practical problems experienced)

Q.2. Which practical problems, if any, have been experienced in arbitration practice involving state enterprises?

Q.2.1. by state enterprises?

Q.2.2. by private enterprises as contractual partners of state enterprises?

Q.2.3. by arbitration institutions?

Q.2.4. by arbitrators?

Question 3 (Determination of the applicable law)

Q.3. For international commercial contracts or arbitrations involving state enterprises, are there any specific considerations – in contract practice, case law or legal literature – on the applicable law?

Q.3.1. regarding conflict of law rules?

Q.3.2. regarding the choice of law by the contractual partners?

Q.3.3. regarding rules of public law?

Q.3.4. regarding sometimes public international law?

Question 4 (The state of substantive law on state enterprises and abitration)

Q.4. In your national law, which types of state enterprises can be distinguished according to:

Q.4.1. legal structure and status?

Q.4.2. practical ownership or control by the state?

Q.4.3. What relevance have the distinctions above with regard to arbitration?

Question 5 (Relevance of being a separate legal entity)

Q.5. For state enterprises that are legal entities separate from the state:

Q.5.1. under which circumstances may this legal separation be disregarded for which legal issues?

Q.5.2. Can a state enterprise claim *force majeure* and lack of responsibility for non-fulfilment of contractual duties, if the state controlling the state enterprise, interferes by act of state?

yes, always

not under certain circumstances and for certain issues (Please explain details and add respective documentation):

Q.5.3. Under which circumstances, if any, can a state enterprise claim immunity:

Q.5.3.1. from jurisdiction of courts?

Q.5.3.2. from arbitration proceedings?

Q.5.3.3. from enforcement of arbitration awards?

Q.5.4. What would be the consequences if fulfilment of the contractual duties by the state enterprise should be against a major national interest?

same consequences as for private enterprises

specific consequences for state enterprises

Question 6 (Enforcement of arbitration awards against state enterprises)

Q.6.1. Is enforcement of arbitration awards against state enterprises possible?

Q.6.2. Are there any legal requirements specific for enforcement against state enterprises?

Q.6.3. Do state enterprises normally fulfil arbitration awards without enforcement?

Question 7 (Suggestions for improvements)

Q.7. What would you suggest as improvements in the field of arbitration involving state enterprises:

Q.7.1. for contract practice?

Q.7.2. for arbitration practice?

Q.7.3. for changes of national law?

Q.7.4. for changes of international law?

Question 8 (Further comments)

Q.8. Which further comments would you like to make regarding:

Q.8.1. arbitration and state enterprises?

Q.8.2. This research and this questionnaire?

D. QUESTIONNAIRE II. ARBITRATION PRACTICE

Questionnaire II, which was sent to institutions and individuals with experience in arbitration, was identical with Questionnaire I, printed above, except that Question 4 had the following wording:

Question 4

All national legal systems contain different types of state enterprises according to legal structure and status and/or practical ownership or control by the state. In which way have these distinctions proved relevant with regard to arbitration?

CHAPTER V

STOCKHOLM SYMPOSIUM*

October 8, 1982

A. PROGRAMME

09.00 Welcome by Mr. Alvar Lindencrona, Chairman of the Swedish National Committee of the International Chamber of Commerce

09.10 Report on present and future activities of the Institute by Mr. Carl-Henrik Winqwist, Secretary-General of the International Chamber of Commerce

10.00 Arbitration and State enterprises by Prof. Dr. Karl-Heinz Böckstiegel Chair of International Business Law, Cologne University

- presentation of the study by the general rapporteur
- first report
- analysis of the answers to the questionnaires.

12.30 Luncheon

14.00 General discussion together with a panel of international lawyers under the Chairmanship of H.E. Gunnar Lagergren, Marshal of the Realm, former President of the Court of Appeal for Western Sweden, Judge of the European Court of Human Rights.

Members of the panel:
Messrs. Karl-Heinz Böckstiegel; Bola Ajibola, Legal Practitioner, Gbadela Chambers, Lagos (Nigeria); William Laurence Craig, Attorney-at-Law, Coudert Brothers, Paris; Yves Derains, Secretary General of the Court of Arbitration of the International Chamber of Commerce; Djamal Lakhdari, Advocate, Algeria

Points for the discussion:
- Practice of state enterprises with regard to agreeing to and participating in arbitration
    - legal restrictions upon state enterprises agreeing to arbitration
    - practical problems experienced
    - determination of the applicable law
    - relevance of being a separate legal entity

* The contributions presented at the Stockholm Colloquium are available in the Documentation of Material received (see Chapter VII of this book).

– enforcement of arbitration awards against state enterprises
– suggestions for improvements.

17.00 End of the meeting

18.00 Reception offered by the Swedish National Committee at Sällskapet Club, Arsenalsgatan 7

B. LIST OF PARTICIPANTS

I. CHAIRMAN OF THE MEETING

Gunnar LAGERGREN, Marshal of the Realm, former President of the Court of Appeal for Western Sweden, Judge of the European Court of Human Rights.

II. SPEAKERS AND MEMBERS OF THE PANEL

Bola Adesumbo AJIBOLA, Legal Practitioner, Lagos; Member of the Executive Committee of the Institute.

Karl-Heinz BÖCKSTIEGEL, Chair of International Business Law, Cologne University; Member of the Academic Council of the Institute.

William Laurence, CRAIG, Attorney-at-Law, Coudert Brothers, Paris; Member of the Academic Council of the Institute.

Yves DERAINS, Secretary General of the Court of Arbitration of the ICC.

Djamal LAKHDARI, Avocat au Barreau d'Alger; Membre du Conseil scientifique de l'Institut.

Alver LINDENCRONA, Chairman of the Swedish National Committee of the ICC; Member of the Academic Council of the Institute.

Carl-Henrik WINQWIST, Secretary General of the ICC; President of the Executive Committee of the Institute.

III. PARTICIPANTS

Algeria

Nouz-Eddine TERKI, Doyen de la Faculté de Droit d'Alger.

Argentina

Mario O. FOLCHI, President of ALADA (Asociation Latino-americana de derecho aeronautico y espacial); Corresponding member of the Institute.

Horacio Alberto GRIGERA NAON, Private International Law Professor; Corresponding member of the Institute.

Austria

Axel FRIEDBERG, Lawyer, Vienna.

Rudolf KRILYSZYN, Attorney-at-Law, Vienna.

Werner MELIS, Director of the Austrian Federal Economic Chamber; Executive Director of the Austrian National Committee of the ICC.

Otto ORTNER, General Counsel, Oesterreichische Kontrollbank AG, Vienna.

Ewald WENINGER, Attorney-at-Law, Vienna.

Belgium

Léon GOFFIN, Professeur à l'Université Catholique de Louvain; Membre correspondant de l'Institut.

Guy HORSMANS, Professeur UCL; Directeur du Centre Interuniversitaire de droit comparé; Avocat au Barreau de Bruxelles.

Alfred HUBERT, Directeur Electrobel, Bruxelles; Membre correspondant de l'Institut.
Marcel HUYS, Président, Centre Belge pour l'Etude et la Pratique de l'Arbitrage National et International (CEPANI).
Guy KEUTGEN, Conseiller juridique, Fédération des Entreprises de Belgique, Bruxelles.
Charley DEL MARMOL, Professeur à la Faculté de Droit de Liège; Membre du Conseil scientifique de l'Institut.
Philippe MATHEI, Directeur, Confédération Nationale de la Construction, Bruxelles.
Lambert MATRAY, Avocat, Matray et associés, Liège; Membre correspondant de l'Institut.
Jan VAN UYTVANCK, Directeur général, Secrétaire général, PETROFINA, Bruxelles; Membre correspondant de l'Institut.

Denmark

Ole LANDO, Professor, Institute of European Market Law, Copenhagen.

Finland

Reino ERMA, Professor of Private Law, Chairman of Board of Arbitration, University of Tampere.
Ulla GYLLING, Acting Secretary General Finland National Committee of the ICC.
Harry HEDMAN, Attorney, Asianajotoimisto H. Hedman Advokatbyrå, Helsinki.
Heikki JOKELA, Professor, University of Helsinki.
Hannu KÄRÄVÄ, Lawyer, Central Chamber of Commerce of Finland, Helsinki.
Timo KARPPINEN, LLM., Head of Department, Central Chamber of Commerce of Finland, Helsinki.
Klaus LAGUS, Attorney-at-Law, Klaus Lagus Law Office, Helsinki.
Antero MOLANDER, Lawyer, Asianajotoimisto Kauppi & Molander, Helsinki.
Mattu TUOHI, Chief Manager, Skopbank, Helsinki.

France

Pierre BELLET, Premier Président Honoraire à la Cour de Cassation de Paris; Membre du Conseil scientifique de l'Institut.
Georges BERLIOZ, Avocat à la Cour, Berlioz et Associés, Paris.
Jean-Claude BORIE, Conseil juridique, Cabinet J.C. Borie, Paris.
René BOURDIN, Directeur des Services administratifs, Compagnie Générale d'Electricité, Paris.
Henri BUTTIN, Conseiller en Opérations Internationales; Expert près la Cour d'Appel de Versailles; Membre correspondant de l'Institut.
Jean-Louis DELVOLVE, Avocat au Barreau de Paris; Membre du Conseil de l'Ordre; SCP Goldsmith, Delvolvé & Associés, Paris.
Frédéric EISEMANN, Secrétaire Général Honoraire, Cour d'arbitrage de la CCI, Paris.
Michel, GAUDET, Président de la Cour d'Arbitrate de la CCI; Président de la Fédération Française des Sociétés d'Assurances; Ancien Directeur Général du Service Juridique de la Commission des Communautés Européennes; Membre du Comité Exécutif de l'Institut.
Berthold, GOLDMAN, Professeur, Université de Paris II; Membre du Conseil scientifique de l'Institut.
Luigi IMPALLOMENI, Avocat, Juriste d'entreprise, Paris.
Serge LAZAREFF, Directeur des Accords & Contrats Internationaux, Péchiney-Ugine-Kuhlmann, Paris.
Danièle LEBORGNE, Direction Département Contrats, TOTAL CFP, Saint-Germain-en-Laye.
Jean LISBONNE, Avocat à la Cour de Paris.
Jean MARION, Conseiller Honoraire à la Cour de Cassation, Membre Titulaire à la Cour Supérieure d'Arbitrage (Conseil d'Etat) Paris.
Jacques MAURO, Avocat à la Cour d'Appel de Paris.
Xavier DE MELLO, Avocat au Barreau de Paris.
Ernst MEZGER, Docteur en Droit, Avocat à la Cour de Paris.
Jean MISIANO, Directeur Export, Trindel, Saint-Ouen.
Bernard DE NERCY, Chef du Département des Affaires Juridiques, Commissariat à l'Energie Atomique, Paris.
Richard NEUER, Avocat à la Cour de Paris.
Dominique ORCEL, Juriste d'entreprise, Paris.
Erik PETERSEN, Chef des Services Juridiques, CGEE-Alsthom.

Gilles PISSEAU, Ingénieur-Expert près la Cour d'Appel et le Tribunal Administratif de Paris; Arbitre-Expert près le Tribunal de Commerce de Paris.
Jean-Paul RETRAINT, Chef du Service Juridique, Fives-Cail Babcock, Paris.
Jean ROBERT, Avocat au Barreau de Paris.
Gilles SILBERMAN, Avocat au Barreau de Paris.
Xavier TANDEAU DE MARSAC, Avocat au Barreau de Paris; Membre correspondant de l'Institut.
Annie TOUBIANA, Professeur à la Faculté de Droit de Paris V.
Michel VILLARD, Avocat à la Cour, Paris.

Germany (Democratic Republic of)

Fritz ENDERLEIN, Director, Institut for Foreign and Comparative Law at the Academy for Political and Legal Science, Potsdam-Babelsberg.

Germany (Federal Republic of)

Menno ADEN, Company Lawyer, Ruhrgas Aktiengesellschaft, Essen.
Arved DERINGER, Attorney-at-Law, Deringer-Tessin-Herrmann & Sedemund; Corresponding member of the Institute.
Ottoarndt GLOSSNER, President of the Commission on International Arbitration of the ICC; Member of the Academic Council of the Institute; Attorney-at-Law, Kronberg.
Franz LASCHET, Attorney-at-Law, German National Committee of the ICC.
Hans Dieter MOSTHAF, Zentralabteilung Recht, Gerlingen-Schillerhöhe.
Timm RIEDINGER, Resident Partner, Curtis Mallet-Prevost, Colt & Mosle, Paris.
Rolf STOEDTER, Chairman, Standing Committee, International Maritime Arbitration Organization (IMAO); Member of the Executive Committee of the Institute; Shipping Company of John T. Essberger, Hamburg.
Christian WIEGAND, Lawyer; General Secretary, Bauindustrieverband Hamburg E.V.
Hanns Ulrich ZSCHIRNT, Attorney-at-Law, Dal Multinational, Eppstein.

Iran

Ali KHADEM, International Lawyer, Law Office Dr. Khadem, Tehran.

Italy

Giorgio BERNINI, Attorney-at-Law; Professor of Commercial Law, University of Bologna; Member of the Academic Council of the Institute.
Mauro RUBINO-SAMMARTANO, Avocat à la Cour, Président du Sous-Comité Section on Business Law, International Bar Association, Milano.

Libya

Nagi, NABBAL, Legal Advisor, National Oil Corporation, New York.
Khalid ELLAFI, Member of the Litigation Department, PO Box 115, Tripoli.

Netherlands

Jan H. DIEPHUIS, Legal Adviser, Royal Dutch Petroleum Company, The Hague.
Pieter SANDERS, Professor, University of Rotterdam; President, Netherlands Arbitration Institute; Member of the Academic Council of the Institute.
Leonard H. W. VAN SANDICK, Partner, Loeff and Van der Ploeg, Rotterdam.
C. C. A. VOSKUIL, Director, TMC Asser Institute, The Hague; Corresponding member of the Institute.

Nigeria

Michael Ayodele AJOMO, Professor of Law, University of Lagos; Corresponding member of the Institute.
Alfred KASUNMU, Professor, University of Lagos; Solicitor & Legal Consultant; Corresponding member of the Institute.

Norway

Haakon E. BØHN, Lawyer, Årdal og Sunndal Verk a.s., Oslo.
Kristian Fredik GRØN, Lawyer, Årdal og Sunndal Verk a.s., Oslo.
Bjørn HAUG, Attorney General (Civil Affairs), Oslo.

Poland

Jan LOPUSKI, Professor, Torun University; Scientific Consultant to Warta Insurance and Reinsurance Company, Torun.

Spain

Bernardo CREMADES, Avocat; Membre du Conseil scientifique de l'Institut.
Julio GONZALEZ-SORIA, Professor of International Law and Lawyer; Member of the Executive Committee and Chairman of the Arbitration Commission – Madrid Chamber of Commerce and Industry.
Fernando POMBO, Senior Partner, Gomez-Acebo & Pombo Abogados, Madrid.

Sweden

Peter AGERMAN, Legal Counsel, Svenska Handelsbanken (Central legal department), Stockholm.
Bo BENELL, Company Lawyer, Saléninvest AB, Stockholm.
Ander BERGNÄS, Legal Counsel ABV, Armerad Betong Vägförbättringar AB, Stockholm.
Stefan BERNHARD, Lawyer, Advokatfirman Lagerlöf, Stockholm.
Ingvar BOMAN, Lawyer, Advokatfirman Palm-Jensen & Roos, Stockholm.
Lars BOMAN, Solicitor, Advokatfirman Morssing & Nycander, Stockholm.
Kathleen BREWINGTON, Partner, Hedberg & Runeland, Stockholm.
Gotthard CALISSENDORFF, Lawyer, Carl Swartling Advokatbyrå, Stockholm.
Hans CARLSTEN, Lawyer, Wetter and Wetter Advokat Byraa, Stockholm.
Anders CHRISTNER, Associate, Alf Lindahl Law Offices, Stockholm.
Karl-Erik DANIELSSON, Lawyer, Advokatfirman Lagerlöf, Stockholm.
Rolf DEULLAR, Department for Legal Affairs, Sveriges Mekanförbund, Stockholm.
Per DINTLER, Jur Kand, Swedish Woodexporters' Association, Stockholm.
Nils EDWALL, Judge – Svea Hovrätt, Stockholm.
Göran EKDAHL, Lawyer, Gedda & Ekdahl Advokat Byraa, Stockholm.
Sven ERSMAN, Attorney-at-Law, Surrey & Morse; National Commissioner, Swedish National Committee of the ICC, Paris.
Ulf FRANKE, Director, Stockholm Chamber of Commerce.
Lars FREDBORG, Attorney-at-Law, Alf Hindahls Advokatbyrå, Stockholm.
Ormonde GOLDIE, Ormonde Goldie Advokatbryå, Stockholm
Lars GORTON, Professor of Law, Salen Shipping Companies, Stockholm.
Lars GÖTHLIN, Company Lawyer, Aktiebolaget Statens Skogsindustrier-ASSIE, Stockholm.
Carl-Åke HEDQVIST, President, Frigoscandia France, Neuilly-sur-Seine.
Emil HEIJNE, Bachelor of Laws, Wetter & Wetter Advokatbyrå, Stockholm.
Hans HERRLIN, Director, Rederi AB Nordstjernan, Stockholm.
Olov HERTZMAN, Legal Adviser, Department of Justice, Stockholm.
Lars HEUMAN, Assistant Professor of Legal Procedure, University of Lund.
Lars A. E. HJERNER, Professor, University of Stockholm; Member of the Academic Council of the Institute.
Mats HILDING, Judge, Law Court of Stockholm.
Christer HOLM, Advocate, Advokatfirman Wesslau, Holm & Co., Stockholm.
Ulf HOLMBÄCK, Lawyer, Stockholm.
Örjan JARVIN, B.L., Stig Rindborg Advokatbyrå, Stockholm.
Carin KÄLLENIUS, LL.B., Stockholm.
Sten KÄLLENIUS, past Man. Dir. of the Swedish Association of General Contractors and House Buildings, Stockholm.
Gunnar KARNELL, Professor of Law, LL.D., Stockholm School of Economics.
Bengst KOSTERMAN, Area-Manager – Eastern Europe, Swedish Trade Council, Stockholm.
Hans KRISTENSEN, Director Chief Consulting Engineer, VBB; Representative of FIDIC, Stockholm.

Per-Anders KULL, Legal Counsel, Sandvik AB, Sandviken.
Martin LAUSSON, Manager Legal Section, Ekn – Exportkreditnaemnden, Swedish Export Credits Guarantee Board, Stockholm.
Erik LIND, Lawyer, Wetter & Wetter Advokatbyrå, Stockholm.
Johan LIND, President, Labour Court, Lidingö.
Gustav LINDENCRONA, Professor, University of Stockholm.
Gunnar LINNANDER, Former Presiding Judge, Stockholm District Court.
Anders LITZÉN, President of Division, Judge Svea Court of Appeal, Stockholm.
Sten LJUNGGREN, LL.B., Stockholm Chamber of Commerce.
Staffan MAGNUSSON, Ministry of Justice, Under Secretary for Legal Affairs, Bromma.
Ulf MAGNUSSON, General Counsel, Electrolux, Stockholm.
Nils MANGÅRD, Judge, Stockholm Chamber of Commerce.
Curt NILSSON, Chairman of the Board, Svenska Vägaktiebolaget Johnson Construction Company AB, Solna.
Ulf NORDENSON, Conseiller à la Cour Suprême de Stockholm.
Björn PALM-JENSEN, Lawyer, Advokatfirman Palm-Jensen & Roos, Stockholm.
Erik AF PETERSÉNS, Lawyer, Setterwall, Kleberg & Co., Stockholm.
Lars RAHM, Lawyer, Mannheimer & Zetterlöf, Göteborg.
Jan RAMBERG, Professor of Commercial Law, University of Stockholm; Member of the Academic Council of the Institute.
Stig RINDBORG, Lawyer, Stig Rindborg Advokatbyrå, Stockholm.
Sten RUDHOLM, President, Svea Court of Appeal, Stockholm.
Per RUNELAND, Lawyer, Hedberg & Runeland Advokatbyrå, Stockholm.
Anders RYDIN, Lawyer, Wetter & Wetter Advokatbyrå, Stockholm.
Maina SANCHO, Legal Counsel, Kooperativa Förbundet, Stockholm.
Stefan SANDÉN, Lawyer, Advokatfirman Lagerlöf, Stockholm.
Sten SILJESTRÖM, Corporate General Counsel, ASEA AB; Corresponding Member of the Institute.
Olle SÖDERSTRÖM, Attorney-at-Law, Advokat Olle Söderström, Stockholm.
Hans STENBERG, Deputy Managing Director, Institute of Foreign Law Ltd., Stockholm.
Jacob SUNDBERG, Professor of Law, University of Stockholm.
Olof WAERN, Attorney-at-Law, G. Sandströms Advokatbyrå, Stockholm.
Kjell WALLÉN, Skanska, Danderyd.
Göran WESTLUND, Legal Counsel, Kooperativa Förbundet (KF), Stockholm.
Gösta WESTRING, Partner, Advokatfirman Cederquist, Stockholm.
Lennart WIBERG, Senior Vice-President General Counsel and Secretary, Saab-Scania AB, Södertälje.

Switzerland

Philippe DE COULON, Avocat, Etude Lenz, Schluep, Briner & De Coulon, Genève.
René HELG, Avocat, Genèva.
Philippe RICHARD, Docteur en droit, avocat, Lausanne.
Verena TRUTMANN, Sous-Directeur, Sandoz S.A., Bâle.
François VERMEILLE, Directeur, ICME Conseils d'entreprises, Zurich; Membre de la Commission de l'Arbitrage International de la CCI.

Syria

Siham AL CHARIF, Directeur, Conseiller financier, Ministère des Finances, Damas.
Sami SARKIS, Docteur en droit, avocat à la Cour de Damas.

Tunisia

Mohamed KCHOUK, Chef du Service Juridique, Entreprise Tunisienne d'Activités Pétrolières, Tunis.
Habib MALOUCHE, Dédlégué général, Association Professionnelle des Banques de Tunisie, Tunis.

Turkey

Rabi KORAL, Professor at the University of Istanbul, Legal Counsel and Delegate of the Chamber of Industry of Istanbul; Corresponding Member of the Institute.

United Kingdom
John CHURCH, Company Solicitor, Cementation International Limited, London.
Martin DAY, Partner, Linklaters & Paines, London.
Michael ELLAND-GOLDSMITH, Barrister & Conseil Juridique, Clifford-Turner, Paris.
Ajmal HAMEED, Lawyer, Kennedys – Law Attorneys, London.
Andrew MARTIN, Professor, London
F. L. DE MAY, Senior Leal Adviser, Shell International Petroleum Company Ltd., London.

United States of America
Axel BAUM, Resident Partner, Hughes Hubbard & Reed, Paris.
John F. CRAWFORD, Partner, Surrey & Morse, Paris; Alternate National Commissioner, United States National Committee of the ICC.
Stuart M. FISCHMAN, Attorney, International Arbitrator and Professor of Law, Moses & Singer, Esqs., New York.
George SPINA, Executive Director, International Law Institute.

Venezuela
Peter Franz SCHRODER DE SCHULZ, Kollontanyi, Graf von Kollontanyi – President, Pandica C.A., Caracas.

Yugoslavia
Dobrosav MITROVIC, Professeur à l'Université de Belgrade.
Zdravko ZDRAVKOVIĆ, Professeur à l'Université de Belgrade.

IV. SWEDISH NATIONAL COMMITTEE

Martin DWORÉN, Secretary General
Ingalill NYMAN, Assistant Secretary General

V. INTERNATIONAL HEADQUARTERS OF THE ICC

Yves DERAINS, Secrétaire Général de la Cour d'Arbitrage.
Xavier GIOCANTI, Secrétaire de l'Institut du Droit et des Pratiques des Affaires Internationales.
Tila Maria DE HANCOCK, Directeur de la Court d'Arbitrage.

VI. OTHERS

Michèle GARZON, Institut du Droit et des Pratiques des Affaires Internationales
Josette WATRIN, Cour d'Arbitrage

CHAPTER VI

BIBLIOGRAPHY AND COLLECTION OF CASES*

A. BIBLIOGRAPHY

* Collected mainly by two assistants to the author at the chair of International Business Law at Cologne University, Dr. Alexander Catranis and Beate Maiwald.

A. BIBLIOGRAPHY

A.1. PUBLICATIONS DEALING WITH THE TOPIC IN GENERAL

American Arbitration Association, 'Arbitration by Governmental Bodies', *Lawyer's Arbitration Letters*, May 15, 1966, 1–13.

Asa'ad, *Commercial Arbitration and Legal System in Kuwait* (Kuwait 1978).

Batiffol, Henri, 'Arbitration Clauses Concluded between French Government-Owned Enterprises and Foreign Private Parties', 7 *Columbia Journal of Transnational Law* 32 (1968).

Batifoll, Henri, *Aspects philosophiques du droit international privé* (Paris 1956).

Bastid/David, *La personalité morale et ses limites* (1960).

Böckstiegel, Karl-Heinz, 'The Relationship between the UNCITRAL Arbitration Rules and the National Law Applicable to the Arbitration', published in German version in RIW (1982) 706.

——, 'Arbitration of disputes between states and private enterprises in the International Chamber of Commerce' 59 *American Journal of International Law* (1965) 579.

——, 'Internationale Schiedsgerichtsbarkeit zwischen Staaten und Privatunternehmen', AWD (1965) 101.

——, *Der Staat als Vertragspartner ausländischer Privatunternehmen* (Frankfurt/Main 1971).

——, 'Arbitration on Contracts between States and Foreign Private Enterprises', in *Collection of the IVth International Congress on Arbitration Materials* (Moscow 1972), p. 670.

——, 'Besondere Probleme der Schiedsgerichtsbarkeit zwischen Privatunternehmen und ausländischen Staaten oder Staatsunternehmen', *Neue Juristische Wochenschrift* (1975) 1577.

——, 'Rechtsschutz der Auslandsinvestitionen durch Schiedsgerichte' lecture before an international colloquium on international investment by the German Federation of Industry, February 22 and 23, 1983. Shortly to be published in the Proceedings of that Colloquium.

——, 'Das anwendbare Recht bei öffentlich-rechtlich geprägten Staatsaufträgen' *Recht der Internationalen Wirtschaft* (1973) 117.

——, *Die allgemeinen Grundsätze des Völkerrechts über Eigentumsentziehung* (Berlin 1963).

——, *Der Staat als Vertragspartner ausländischer Privatunternehmen* (Frankfurt 1971).

——, 'Specific Problems of International Arbitration between States and Private Enterprises' in *Proceedings of the Vth International Arbitration Congress* (New Delhi 1975), C, III, e, pp. 1–12.

——, *Die internationale Schiedsgerichtsbarkeit in der Schweiz* (Köln 1979).

——, *Vertragspraxis und Streiterledigung im Wirtschaftsverkehr mit arabischen Staaten*, Schriftenreihe des Deutschen Instituts für Schiedsgerichtswesen, Band 2 (Köln/Berlin/Bonn/München 1981).

——, 'Die internationale Handelsschiedsgerichtsbarkeit in Österreich', *Neue Juristische Wochenschrift* (1981) 501.

——, 'Besonder Aspekte der Wirtschaftsschiedsgericht barkeit mit Parteien aus Entwicklungsländern', *Neue Juristische Wochenschrift* (1981) 1862.

Borchers, *Verträge von Staaten mit ausländischen Privatpersonen* (Göttingen 1966)

Braucher, 'Arbitration Under Government Contracts' 17 *Law & Contemporary Problems* (1952) 473.

Burkhardt, Hans-Martin, 'Die Verhandlungen über eine Investitionsschutzkonvention im Rahmen des Euro-arabischen Dialogs' *Recht der Internationalen Wirtschaft* (1983) 164.

Carabiber, Charles, 'L'arbitrage international entre Gouvernments et particuliers', *Recueil des Cours Académie de Droit International* 76 (1950 I) 221.

——, 'L'arbitrage international et la réserve de l'ordre public', *Revue de l'Arbitrage* (1956) 118.

——, 'Les tribunaux internationaux et les Intérets Privés', *Etudes de Droit Contemporain, Institut de Droit Comparé de l'université de Paris XV* (1959) 305.

Catranis, Alexander, 'Probleme der Nationalisierung ausländischer Unternehmen vor internationalen Schiedsgerichten – Die libyschen Streitfälle, *Recht der Internationalen Wirtschaft* (1982) 19.

Centre de Recherche sur le Droit des Marches et des Investissements Internationaux (Dijon), *Investissement Etrangers et Arbitrage Entre Etats et Personnes Privées* (Dijon 1969).

Cogan, John P., 'Are Government Bodies Bound by Arbitration Agreements? An Eastman Arbitration Library Prize-Winning Essay' 22 *Arbitration Journal* (1967) 151. (Corporations with some government control but primarily created for profit should be bound by arbitration agreements.)

Cohn, Ernest, Domke, Martin, Eisemann, Frédéric, *Handbook of Institutional Arbitration in International Trade. Facts, Figures and Rules* (Amsterdam/New York/Oxford 1977).

——, *Commercial Arbitration, Essays in Memoriam Eugenio Minoli* (Turin 1974).

Cohn, E. J., Simitis, C., ' "Lifting of the Veil" in the Company Laws of the European Continent', 12 *International and Comparative Law Quarterly* (1963) 189.

Delaume, Georges, *Transnational Contracts Applicable Law and Settlement of Disputes* (New York 1980).

——, 'State Contracts and Transnational Arbitration', 75 *American Journal of International Law*, (1981) 784.

——, 'Foreign sovereign immunity: impact on arbitration', *The Arbitration Journal* (June 1983) 34.

Derains, Yves, 'Le statut des usages du commerce international devant les juridictions arbitrales', *Revue de l'arbitrage* (1973) 122.

Domke, Martin, 'Arbitration of State-Trading Relations', *Law & Contemporary Problems* (1959) 317. (General considerations of east-west arbitration; review and critique of the *Lena Goldfields* case.)

——, 'Arbitration between Governmental Bodies and Foreign Private Firms', 17 *Arbitration Journal* (1962) 129.

——, 'Arbitration Between Government-Controlled Bodies and Foreign Business Firms', *International Law Association Report on the Fiftieth Conference in Brussels* (1962/1963) 253.

——, 'Arbitration between Government-Controlled Bodies and Foreign Business Firms', *International Law Association – Helsinki Conference 1966*, 6 pages.

——, 'Recent Development in International Commercial Arbitration', 2 *New York University Journal of International Law & Politics* (1969) 267.

——, 'New Aspects of East-West Trade Arbitration' in *Commercial Arbitration – Essays in Memoriam Eugenion Minoli*, (Turin 1974), p. 121.

——, 'Progress Report for the Committee on International Arbitration between Government-Controlled Bodies and Foreign-Owned Business Firms' in *International Law Association, Report of the Fifty-Sixth Conference held at New Delhi* (London 1976), p. 524. (A general survey of the subject.)

——, 'Arbitration between Government-Controlled Bodies and Foreign-Owned Business Firms' in *International Law Association, Report of the Fifty-Seventh Conference held at Madrid* (London 1978), p. 33.

Dunshee de Abranches, C., *Proceedings, VIth International Arbitration Congress* (Mexico City 1978).

Durand, Paul, 'Le règlement par voie de transactions et d'arbitrage des differends de droit privé intéressant les établissements publics de caractère industriel et commercial', *Droit Social* (1949), p. 325.

Eisemann, Frédéric, 'The Present Situation of International Commercial Arbitration between States or State Entities and Foreign Private Parties', Report presented at the Fifth Congress on International Commercial Arbitration held in New Delhi in January 1975.

Eisemann, Frédéric, Melis, Werner, *INCOTERMS (Commentary)* (Vienna 1980).

Fellhauer, Harry, Strohbach, Heinz, *Handbuch der internationalen Handelsschiedsgerichtsbarkeit*, in vier Bänden, (East Berlin, 1969).

Fischer, Peter, 'Das internationale Unternehmen als Phänomen in der Völkerrechtsgeschichte Völkerrecht und Rechtsphilosophie', *Internationale Festschrift für Stephan Verosta zum 70. Geburtstag* (Berlin 1980), p. 345.

——, *Die internationale Konzession*. Theorie und Praxis der Rechtsinstitute in den internationalen Wirtschaftsbeziehungen. Mit einem Verzeichnis internationaler Konzessionsverträge. (Wien 1974).

Flamme, M. A., 'L'arbitrage dans les relations entre personnes de droit public et personnes de droit privé', 20 *Recueil de jurisprudence du droit administratif et du conceil d'Etat* (1965) 232.
Flamme, Maurice-André, Horsmans, Guy, 'L'arbitrage dans les rapports entre personnes de droit public et personnes de droit privé', in *Travaux du deuxième Congrès International de l'Arbitrage* (Rotterdam July 6–9, 1966). *Revue de l'Arbitrage* (1966) numéro spécial, p. 85. (Comparative survey with special regard to French and Belgian practice.)
Friedmann, W., *Legal Theory* (London 1960).
Geiger, Rainer, 'The Unilateral Change of Economic Development Agreement' 23 *International & Comparative Law Quarterly* (1974) 73.
Goldman, Berthold, 'La lex mercatoria dans les contracts et l'arbitrage internationaux: réalité et perspectives', 106 *Clunet* (1979) 475.
——, *Frontières du droit et lex mercatoria, Archives de philosophie du droit* (Paris 1964).
Graham, 'The Calvo Clause: Its Current Status as a Contractual Renunciation of Diplomatic Protection, 6 Texas ILR (1971) 289.
Grzybowski, Kazimierz (ed.), 'East-West Trade: Part I' 37 *Law & Contemporary Problems* (1972) 393.
——, 'East-West Trade: Part II', 37 *Law & Contemporary Problems* (1972) 533.
Haalck, Jürgen, 'Zum gegenwärtigen Stand der Schiedsgerichtsbarkeit im Bereich der intersystemaren Wirtschaftsbeziehungen', *Recht im Außenhandel* (1975), pp. 1–5.
Haight, James T. (ed.), *Current Legal Aspects of doing Business with Sino-Soviet Nations,* Proceedings of an American Bar Association Annual Meeting Program of the Section of International Law, held in San Francisco, California on August 15, 1972.
Holtzmann, Howard M., 'Settlements of Disputes: The Role of Arbitration in East-West Trade', in Starr (ed.), *East-West Business Transactions* (New York . . . 1974), p. 540.
Holzman, Franklyn D., *International Trade under Communism – Politics and Economics* (New York 1976). (Theory of foreign trade institutions and behaviour of centrally planned economies; east-west economic relations.)
Hübner, Ulrich, 'Der Durchgriff bei juristischen Personen im europäischen Gesellschafts- und Unternehmensrecht', *Juristen Zeitung* (1978) 703.
International Law Association, *Proceedings of the Conferences 1960 to 1978.*
Jakubowski, J., 'Arbitration in the CMEA', London Conference on International Commercial Arbitration (October 1974), 12 pages, unpublished. (East-west Arbitration; Moscow Convention 1972; CMEA general conditions.)
Jennings, R. Y., 'State Contracts in International Law', 37 *British Yearbook of International Law* (1961) 156.
Jimenez de Arechaga, Eduardo, *L'arbitrage entre les états et les sociétés privées étrangères, Hommages au Professeur Gilbert Gidel* (1958).
Kiesewetter, Bruno, *Der Ostblock. Außenhandel des östlichen Wirtschaftsblockes einschließlich China* (Berlin 1960).
Kos – Rabcewicz – Zubkowski, *East European Rules on the Validity of International Commercial Arbitration Agreements* (London 1970).
——, 'Arbitration Agreements and Adjudication of East-West Economic Disputes', in *Proceedings of the Vth Intern. Arbitr. Congress* (New Delhi 1975), C, I, e, pp. 1–25.
Lalive, Jan Flavien, 'Contracts between a State or a State Agency and a Foreign Company', 13 *International & Comparative Law Quarterly* (1964) 987.
——, 'Contrats entre Etats ou Entreprises Etatiques et Personnes Privées' RdC (1980), Section X et XI.
Lalive, Pierre, 'L'Etat ou tant que partie à des contracts de concession ou d'investissements conclus avec des sociétés privées étrangères', in *New Directions in International Trade Law*, vol. I, Reports, pp. 317–373.
Löber, Heinz H., 'Die Durchbrechung der Rechtspersönlichkeit bei Kapitalgesellschaften in den Rechten Österreichs, Deutschlands und der USA', *Zeitschrift für Rechtsvergleichung* (1966) 61.
Mann, F. A., 'State Contracts and International Arbitration', 42 *British Yearbook of International Law I* (1967).
——, 'Theoretical Approach towards the Law Governing Contracts between States and Private Persons', *Revue belge de droit international* (1975) 586.

——, 'The Proper Law of Contracts conducted by International Persons', 35 *British Yearbook of International Law* (1959) 34.

McLaughlin, Joseph T., 'Arbitration and Developing Countries', 13 *The International Lawyer* (1979) 211.

McNair, 'The General Principles of Law Recognized by Civilized Nations', 33 *British Yearbook of International Law* (1957) 1.

Melis, Werner, 'East-West Arbitration, in *Hommages Eisemann*, p. 97. (General problems relating to this subject.)

Mestre, Achille, 'Les Etablissements Publics Industriels et Commerciaux et le Recours à l'Arbitrage' (L'apport de l'art. 7 de la loi 75–596 du 9 juillet 1975) *Revue de l'Arbitrage* (1976) 3. (Critical remarks on the prohibition to public enterprises to submit to arbitration; survey over doctrine and jurisprudence in France; the new law 75–596 of 9.7.1975 and its impact on arbitration and public enterprises.)

Motulsky, H., 'L'arbitrage commercial et les personnes morales du droit public', *Revue de l'Arbitrage* (1956) 38.

——, 'La capacité de compromettre des Etablissements publics à caractère commercial. A Propos de l'arret "Société Nationale de Vente des Surplus" ', *Revue de l'Arbitrage* (1958) 39.

Note, 'Authority of Government Corporations to Submit Disputes to Arbitration', 49 *Columbian Law Review* (1949) 97.

O'Connell, D. P., *International Law*, esp. Volume II, Part 10: 'International Litigation' (London 1970).

Oppetit, Bruno, 'Eléments pour une sociologie de l'arbitrage', 27 *L'année sociologique* (1976) 179.

Pfaff, Dieter, 'Die Außenhandelsschiedsgerichtsbarkeit der sozialistischen Länder im Handel mit der BRD', *Schriftenreihe Recht der intern. Wirtschaft*, Bd. 7 (Heidelberg 1973).

Rengeling, Hans-Werner, *Privatvölkerrechtliche Verträge* (Berlin 1971).

Ribolzi, C., 'The Choice and Appointment of Board of Arbitrators in Disputes Concerning Public Works in Local Public Bodies' in *Commercial Arbitration – Essays in Memoriam Eugenio Minoli* (Turin 1974), p. 425.

Rigaux, Francois, *Droit public et droit privé dans les relations internationales*. Publications de la Revue Générale de Droit International Public, Nouvelle Série – No. 26 (Paris (Pedone) 1977).

Rubin (ed.), *Foreign Development Lending – Legal Aspects* (1971).

Sacerdoti, G., *I contrati tra Stati e stranieri nel diritto internazionale* (Milano 1972).

Sanders, P., 'Trade Arbitration between East and West', 15 *International & Comparative Law Quarterly* (1966) 718.

Schlesinger, Rudolf B., Gündisch, Herbert-Jürgen, 'Allgemeine Rechtsgrundsätze als Rechtsnormen in Schiedsverfahren – Ein Beitrag zur Theorie der Endnationalisierung von Verträgen', 28 RabelsZ (1964) 4.

Schlosser, Peter, 'Schiedsgerichtsbarkeit und öffentlichrechtlich beeinflußte Streitgegenstände in *Festschrift für Arthur Bülow* (München 1981), p. 189.

Seidl-Hohenveldern, Ignaz, 'Souveränität und wirtschaftliche Koexistenz, 86 *Clunet* (1959) 1050.

Sierra, Humberto Briseno, *El Arbitraje Comercial* (Mexico 1979).

Ssekandi, Francis M., 'Contracts between a State and a Foreign Private Company. Reflections on the Effectiveness of the Arbitration Process', 2 *East African Law Journal*, No. 4, Dec. 1966.

Stalev, Zhirko, Practical Applications in the Field of Arbitration in Private Exchanges between East and West, Relation in the International Meeting on Arbitration, Cours 21./22. May 1981, organized by the Camera di Commercio, Industria Astigianato ed Agricoltura

Standke, Klaus Heinrich, 'Der Handel mit dem Osten. Die Wirtschaftsbeziehungen mit den Staatshandelsländern' *Schriftenreihe zum Handbuch für Europäische Wirtschaft*, Band 36 (Baden-Baden 1968).

Starr, Robert, *East-West Business Transactions* (New York/Washington/London 1974). (The book is divided into three parts: (1) regulation of east-west business transactions by market economy countries, with reports from the USA, Japan, EEC, FRG and the UK; (2) organization and conduct of foreign trade in countries with state-planned economies, with reports from the COMECON, Bulgaria, CSSR, GDR, Hungary, Poland, Romania, the USSR, Yugoslavia and the People's Republic of China; (3) several aspects of east-west transactions.)

Stoll, Jutta, *Vereinbarungen zwischen Staat und ausländischem Investor* (Berlin 1982).
——, 'Rechtsnatur und Bestandsschutz von Vereinbarungen zwischen Staaten und ausländischen privaten Investoren' in *Recht der internationalen Wirtschaft* (1981) p. 808.
Storme, M., 'L'arbitrage entre personnes de droit public et personnes de droit privé, *Revue de l'Arbitrage* (1978) 113.
Straus, Donald B., 'The growing consensus on International Commercial Arbitration', 68 *American Journal of International Law* (1974) 709.
Strohbach, Heinz, *Rechtsverfolgung und Streitbeilegung in den internationalen Wirtschaftsbeziehungen mit dem NWS*, (Berlin, Hochschule für Ökonomie, 1979).
——, 'Study on the Perfection of the Existing Mechanism for the Settling of Commercial Disputes', in *Industry 2000 – New Perspectives, Collected Background Papers*, Vol. 2: International Industrial Enterprises (Vienna 1979), pp 261–280.
The USSR Chamber of Commerce and Industry (ed.), *Collection of the IVth International Congress on Arbitration Materials*, 3–6 October 1972 (Moscow).
Vedel, Georges, 'Le problème de l'arbitrage entre gouvernements ou personnes de droit public et personnes de droit privé', *Revue de l'Arbitrage* (1961) 116. (A survey over national (french) law and propositions for a development.)
Veith, Werner, Böckstiegel, Karl-Heinz, *Der Schutz von ausländischem Vermögen im Völkerrecht* (Studien zum Europäischen Wirtschaftsrecht, Bd 4).
Vuylsteke, C., 'Foreign Investment Protection and ICSID Arbitration' 4 GeJl & CL (1974) 343.
Wetter, J. Gilles, *The International Arbitral Process: Public and Private*, Five volumes, (New York 1979).
Zweigert, Konrad, 'Verträge zwischen staatlichen und nichtstaatlichen Partnern', in *Berichte der Deutschen Gesellschaft für Völkerrecht*, Bd 5 (1963).
Zourek, Joroslav, 'Some comments on the difficulties encountered in the juridical settlement of disputes arising from trade between countries with different economic and social structure', 86 *Clunet* (1959) 639.

A.2. PUBLICATIONS DEALING WITH CERTAIN ASPECTS OF THE TOPIC

A.2.1. Reports and comments on cases

Becker, Joseph, 'The ROLIMPEX Exit from International Contract Responsibility', 10 *New York University Journal of International Law and Politics* (1978) 447.
Berg, Albert Jan van den, 'Comparative Table *Topco* v. *Libya* and *B.P.* v. *Libya*' in *Yearbook Commercial Arbitration*, Volume V (1980), p. 161.
Berman, Harold J., 'Force majeure and the Denial of an Export License under Soviet Law: A Comment on *Jordan Investments Ltd.* v. *Soiusnefteksport*', 73 *Harvard Law Review* (1960) 1128.
Carabiber, Ch., 'Chronique sur un arret', *Revue de l'arbitrage* (1966) 93. (Remarks on the *Galakis* case.)
Catranis, Alexander, 'Probleme der Nationalisierung ausländischer Unternehmen vor internationalen Schiedsgerichten – Die libyschen Schiedsfälle', *Recht der Internationalen Wirtschaft*, (1982) 19.
Faragó, L., 'Decisions of the Hungarian Chamber of Commerce in "COMECON" Arbitrations', 14 *International & Comparative Law Quarterly* (1965) 1124.
Hecht, Ariel, 'Einstellung sowjetischer Öllieferungen nach Israel.' Entscheidung der Außenhandels- Arbitragekommission bei der Handelskammer der UdSSR in Moskau. *Außenwirtschaftsdienst* (1958), 187.
——, 'Noch ein Wort zur israelisch- sowjetischen Öl- Arbitrage', *Außenwirtschaftsdienst* (1959) 36.
Lalive, Jean Flavien, 'Un récent arbitrage suisse entre un organisme d'Etat et une société privée étrangère', 19 *Swiss Yearbook of International Law* (1962) 273. (Remarks on the *Sapphire* arbitration.)
——, 'Un grand arbitrage pétrolier entre un Gouvernement et deux sociétés privées étrangères, *Arbitrage Texaco/Calasiatic* c. *Gouvernement Libyen*', *Clunet* (1977) 319.

Lalive, Pierre, 'Arbitrage international et ordre public suisse. Une suprenante décision du Tribunal fédéral: l'arret *SGTM/Bangladesh'*, *Zeitschrift für schweizerisches Recht* 97 neue Folge (1978) I, p. 529. (Dissolution of a state enterprise in order to escape submission to arbitration; critique against an award of the Swiss federal tribunal holding that it does not violate Swiss public order.)

——, Arbitrage international. Dissolution de sociétés. Succession universelle. Substitution de parties. Effets de mesures étatiques étrangères. Ordre public. Note: Trib. fédéral, 5.5.1976, Genève; *Société des grands travaux de Marseille République populaire de Bangladesh et Bangladesh Industrial Development Corporation*, ATF 102 Ia 574 in 34 *Schweizerisches Jahrbuch für Internationales Recht* (1978), p. 392.

Lesser, M., '*Rolimpex (sic.) (C Czarnikow Ltd.* v. *Centrale Handlu Zagraniczuego 'Rolimpex'* [1978] 1 All ER 81): a sweet solution to legal status', 128 *New Law Journal* 59.

MacCrate, Robert, Remarks at the 67th Annual Meeting of the American Society of International Law to the subject: 'Recovering Confiscated Assets and Capturing Sanctioned Goods: Extant and Prospective Remedies' in American Society of International Law (ed.), *Proceedings of the 67th Annual Meeting* (Washington DC 1974), p. 73.

Motulski, Henri, 'La capacité de compromettre des Etablissements publics á caractère commercial (A propos de l'arret, *Société National de Vente des Surplus*)', *Revue de l'Arbitrage* (1958) 39.

Nussbaum, 'The Arbitration between Lena Goldfields Ltd. and the Soviet Government', 36 *Cornell Law Quarterley* (1950) 31.

Pick, Rudolf, 'Einstellung sowjetischer Öllieferungen nach Israel', Entscheidung der Außenhandels Arbitragekommission bei der Handelskammer der UdSSR in Moskau, *Außenwirtschaftsdienst* (1958) 209.

Pisar, Samuel, 'The Communist System of Foreign-trade Adjucation, 72 *Harvard Law Review* (1959) 1409.

Rambaud, Patrick, 'Les Suites d'un différend pétrolier: L'affaire LIAMCO devant le juge français', *Annuaire Française de Droit International* (1979) 820.

Rigaux, Francois, *Droit public et droit privé dans les relations internationales.* Publications de la Revue Générale de Droit International Public, Nouvelle Série – No. 26 (Paris (Pedone) 1977).

Sassoon, 'The Soviet-Israel Oil Arbitration', 3 *The Journal of Business Law* (1959) 132.

Schwebel, Stephen M., 'The Alsing Case' 8 *International & Comparative Law Quarterly* (1959) 329.

Suratgar, 'The Sapphire Arbitration Award', 3 *Columbia Journal of Transnational Law* (1964) 152.

Verdross, Alfred, 'Zwei Schweizer Schiedssprüche über quasi völkerrechtliche Verträge', 21 *Schweizerisches Jahrbuch für Internationales Recht* (1964) 15.

Wengler, Wilhelm, 'Nouveaux aspects de la problematique des contrats entre état et personnes privées', XIV *Revue belge de droit international* (1978–79) 415.

Wolff von Amerongen, Otto (ed.), *Rechtsfragen der Integration und Kooperation in Ost und West* Berlin (1976).

A.2.2. Practical problems experienced

Becker, Elmar, *Die Rechtssprechung der sowjetischen Außenhandelsschiedsrichtskommission*, FIW – Schriftenreihe Heft 17 (Köln . . . 1964).

Böckstiegel, Karl-Heinz (ed.), *Vertragspraxis und Streiterledigung im Wirtschaftsverkehr mit arabischen Staaten*, Schriftenreihe des Deutschen Instituts für Schiedsgerichtswesen, Band 2 (Köln/Berlin/Bonn/München 1981).

Bratous, S. N., 'Force Majeure en tant que motif de dégagement de la responsabilité dans les contrats du commerce extérieur' in *Arbitrage Commercial – Essais in memoriam Eugenion Minoli* (Turin 1974), 57.

Carabiber, Charles, 'L'arbitrage international et le problème de l'immunité de juridiction des états et des collectivités publiques signataires d'une clause compromissoire insérée dans un contrat de droit privé', *Revue de l'Arbitrage* (1967) 49.

Costa, Marie Martins, 'The Competence of the International Court of Justice in Cases Where the Parties Are the Sovereign States and Juridicial Persons', 12 *New York Law Forum*, 280.

Delaume, Georges A., 'State Contracts and Transnational Arbitration', AJIL (1981) 809.

Fellhauer, Harry, *Der Außenhandelskaufmann und die Schiedsgerichte*, Schriftenreihe Rechtsfragen des Außenhandels, Heft 1, Kammer für Außenhandel der DDR (Berlin 1959). (Socialist institutional foreign trade arbitration; procedure and applicable law.)

Friedmann, W. G., 'Changing Social Agreements in State trading States and Their Effect on International Law', 24 *Law & Contemporary Problems* (1959) 350.

Gesang, Jochen, *Force Majeure* (Königstein 1980).

Holtzmann, Howard M., 'New Uses for Arbitration in Soviet-American Contracts for Industrial, Scientific and Technical Development', Report in the *Conference of Soviet-American Trade and its Legal Problems* sponsored by the Carnegie Endowment for International Peace and the American Society for International Law, New York, January 6–11, 1974 (unpublished).

Khadjavi-Gontard, Bardia, Hausmann, Rainer, 'Zurechenbarkeit von Hoheitsakten und subsidiäre Staatshaftung bei Verträgen mit ausländischen Staatsunternehmen' *Recht der Internationalen Wirtschaft/Außenwirtschaftsdienst des Betriebsberaters* (1980) 533. ('Force majeure' and state enterprises: liability of the state for the activity of a state enterprise only if the state *abuses* the separate legal personality of the enterprise. First Group: The state controls the enterprise. Second group: The state acts in order to hinder the performance of a contract.)

Lazare, 'La procedure arbitrale dans les contrats internationaux de travaux publics' in *Arbitrage Commercial – Essais in memoriam Eugenio Minoli* (Turin 1974), p. 273.

Mina-Romer, Catherine, 'L'arbitrage de la commission d'arbitrage pour le commerce exterieur de Moscow dans le commerce Est-Ouest', *Annuaire de l'U.R.S.S. et des pays socialistes européens* (1978) 271.

Note, 'Arbitration Clause for Optional Use in U.S.A.-U.S.S.R. Trade' in III *Yearbook Commercial Arbitration* (1978), p. 299.

Ommeslaghe, Pierre van, 'Les clauses de force majeure et d'imprévision (hardship) dans les contrats internationaux', 57 *Revue droit international droit comparé*, (1980) 7. (Comparative survey of British, American, German, French, Belgian, Swiss, Italian, Spanish and Soviet law; analysis of *force majeure* clauses: enumeration of cases; analysis of hardship clauses; legal consequences; draft of *force majeure* clause.)

Pfuhl, 'Gewährleistung und Garantie im zwischenstaatlichen Außenhandel des Ostblocks' *Recht in Ost und West* (1958) 116.

Przetacznik, Franziszek, 'The sovereign immunity of foreign states and international commercial arbitration', *Revue de droit international de sciences diplomatiques et politiques* (1979) 188.

Recent Development (T. A. Peterson/H. W. Hoyt), 'Foreign Sovereign Immunity', 9 *Georgia Journal of International and Comparative Law* (1979) 111.

'Schiedsvereinbarungen mit Geschäftspartnern in der Sowjetunion', *Außenwirtschaftsdienst* (1959) 218.

Singer, Michael, 'The Act of State Doctrine of the United Kingdom: An Analysis, With comparisons To United States Practice', 75 *American Journal of International Law* (1981) 283.

Sohn/Baxter, 'Responsibility of States for injuries to the economic interests of aliens', 55 *American Journal of International Law* (1961) 545.

Sokolow, Nicolas, 'La force majeure dans les contrats entre sociétés occidentales et centrales commerciales sovietiques', 4 *Droit et pratique du commerce international* (1978) 323. (Decisions of the Soviet Government refusing authorizations or prohibiting performance of a contract are often stipulated as a case of *force majeure*.)

Stargardt, Monika, 'Aspekte der Klausal "unabwendbare Gewalt" in intersystemaren Wirtschaftsverträgen, *Recht im Außenhandel* (1979) 1.

Starr, Robert, Introductory Note on Contracting with Enterprises in State-Planned Economies in Starr (ed.), *East-West Business Transactions* (New York . . . 1974), p. 449.

Verdross, Alfred, 'The Status of Foreign Private Interests Stemming from Economic Development Agreements with Arbitration Clauses' 9 *Österreichische Zeitschrift für öffentliches Recht* (1958/59) 449.

Waehler, Jan Peter, 'Neue Entwicklungen in der Praxis der internationalen Schiedsgerischtsbarkeit im Ost-West-Handel' *Ost-Panorama* Sonderausgabe (Austria 1978), p. 157.

A.2.3. Determination of the applicable law

'Applicable Law in Relations between Intergovernmental Organizations and Private Parties', Hague Academy of International Law, *Recueil des Cours*, vol. III (1967), pp. 426–616.

Böckstiegel, Karl-Heinz, 'Arbitration of disputes between states and private enterprises in the International Chamber of Commerce', 59 *American Journal of International Law* (1965) 579.

——, 'Das anwendbare Recht bei öffentlichrechtlich geprägten Staatsaufträgen', *Außenwirtschaftsdienst/Recht der Internationalen Wirtschaft* (1973) 117.

——, 'Die Bestimmung des anwendbaren Rechts in der Praxis internationaler Schiedsgerichtsverfahren' in *Festschrift für G. Beitzke* (Berlin/New York 1979), p. 443. (Practical problems of the applicable law in international arbitration; special reference to the applicable substantial law; applicable law if a state is party of a contract; application of public law.)

——, 'The Relationship between the UNCITRAL Arbitrational Rules and the National Law Applicable to the Arbitration'. Published in German version RIW (1982) 483.

——, 'Das anwendbare Recht bei öffentlichrechtlichen geprägten Staatsaufträgen', *Recht der Internationalen Wirtschaft* (1973) 117.

Broches, A., 'The Convention on the Settlements of Investment Disputes between States and Nationals of Other States: applicable Law and Default Procedure' in *International Arbitration, Liber Amicorum for Martin Domke* (The Hague 1967), p. 12.

——, 'Choice-of-Law Provisions in Contracts with Governments', 26 *The Record* (1971).

Brumbaugh, Granville M., 'Choice of Law Provisions in Licensing Contracts' in Willis L. M. Reese (ed.) *International Contracts* (New York 1962).

Capatina, Octavian, 'La loi applicable à la convention arbitrale de commerce extérieur', 20 *Revue roumaine des sciences socialessérie de sciences juridiques* (1976) 47.

Eisemann, F., 'La situation actuelle de l'arbitrage commercial international entre Etats ou entités étatiques et personnes physiques ou morales étrangères de droit privé', *Revue de l'Arbitrage* (1975) 292.

Fensterwald, 'The Effect of State Trading Upon Arbitration', 5 *Arbitration Journal* 163 (1950).

Gause, Hermann, Melsheimer, Klaus, 'Beiträge zum sowjetischen Außenhandelsrecht' Berichte des Osteuropa-Instituts an der Freien Universität Berlin – Reihe *Wirtschaft und Recht*, Heft 63 (Berlin 1964). (Principles of arbitration in the USSR; application of foreign law in foreign-trade cases; principles of private international law: validity of choice-of-law clauses.)

Houtte, H. van, 'La loi applicable a l'arbitrage commercial international, 57 *Revue droit international droit comparé* (1980) 285.

Institut de Droit International, *Session d'Athen, Annuaire 58* (1979).

Jakubowski, Jerzy, 'Les problèmes de la loi applicable et de l'arbitrage dans la coopération industrielle entre l'est et l'ouest' in *Hommages Eisemann*, p. 103.

——, 'Les entreprises d'état polonaises dans le commerce international (problèmes juridiques)' in *Problemi giuridici dell' impressa, Colloguio promosso dell Academia Nazionale dei Lincei* in collaborazione con l'Universita di Varsavia (Roma, 24–25 nov. 1975), (Academia Nazionale dei Lincei Roma 1976), p. 87.

Jennings, R. Y., 'State Contracts in International Law', 37 *British Yearbook of International Law* (1961).

Lalive, Pierre, 'Sur une notion de "Contrat international"' in *Multum non Multa, Festschrift für Kurt Lippstein* (Heidelberg/Karlsruhe 1980), p. 135.

——, 'L'Etat ou tant que partie à des contrats de concession ou d'investissements conclus avec des sociétés privées étrangères', *New Direction in Internatonal Trade Law*, vol. I, Reports, pp. 317–373.

Lew, Julian D. M., *Applicable Law in International Commercial Arbitration*, A Study in Commercial Arbitration Awards (New York, 1978).

Mann, F. A., 'The Law Governing State Contracts' *British Yearbook of International Law* (1944) 21.

——, 'The Proper Law of Contracts Concluded by International Persons', 35 *British Yearbook of International Law* (1959) 34.

——, 'State Contracts and International Arbitration', 42 *British Yearbook of International Law* (1967).

Orban, Frank A., 'The Challenge To The Enforcement Of Socialist Arbitral Awards', 17 *Vanderbilt Journal of International Law* (1977) 375. (Growing importance of arbitration in socialist countries; voluntary obeiance to arbitral awards; applicable law.)

Pisar, Samuel, 'Soviet Conflict of Laws in International Commercial Transactions', 70 *Harvard Law Review* (1957) 593.

——, *Praxis des Osthandels*, Übersetzung und Bearbeitung Dr. Karl Lang (Frankfurt/New York 1973). (Judicial status of trade institutions; *force majeure*; relevance of being a separate legal entity; performance of contracts; law applicable in arbitration proceedings.)

Rey, 'Law Governing Contracts between States and Foreign Nationals', 2 *Proceedings of the Institute on Private Investments Abroad* (1960) 5.

Rigaux, Francois, *Droit public et droit privé dans les relations internationales*. Publications de la Revue Générale de Droit International Public, Nouvelle Série – No. 26 (Paris (Pedone) 1977).

——, 'Souveraineté des États et arbitrage transnational' in *Le Droit des Relations Economique Internationales*, Etudes offertes à Berthold Goldman (Paris 1982), p. 261.

Rubin (ed.), *Foreign Development Lending – Legal Aspects* (1971).

Sacerdoti, G., *I contrati tra Stati e stranieri nel diritto internazionale* (Milano 1972).

Smedresman, Peter S., 'Conflict of Laws in International Commercial Arbitration: A Survey of Recent Developments', 7 *California Western International Law Journal* (1977) 263. (A general analysis of conflict of laws problems in arbitration cases with special regard to English and American practice.)

Sornarajah, M., 'The Myth of International Contract Law', *Journal of World Trade Law* (1981) 187.

Stalev, Zhivko, Practical Application in the Field of Arbitration in Private Exchanges between East and West, Relation in the International Meeting on Arbitration, Como 21 and 22 May, 1981. (Not published but available at the Cologne University Chair of International Business Law.)

Stumpf, Herbert, Lindstaedt, Wolfgang, 'Vereinbarungen über das anzuwendende Recht und das zuständige Schiedsgericht in Handelsverträgen mit osteuropäischen Ländern', *Außenwirtschaftsdienst* (1972) 228.

Van Hecke, Georges, *Les accords entre un Etat et une privée étrangère* (Geneva 1977).

Verdross, Alfred, 'The Status of Foreign Private Interests Stemming from Economic Development Agreements with Arbitration Clauses', 9 *Österreichische Zeitschrift für öffentliches Recht*, (1958/59) 449.

——, 'Quasi-International Agreements and International Economic Transactions', 18 *The Yearbook of World Affairs* (1964) 230.

——, 'Zwei Schweizer Schiedssprüche über quasivölkerrechtliche Verträge, 21 *Schweizerisches Jahrbuch für Internationalies Recht* (1964) 15.

Waehler, Jan Peter, 'Die Außenhandels- und See- Schiedsgerichtsbarkeit in der UdSSR. Institutionen, Verfahren und Ermittlung des anwendbaren Rechts', Osteuropa – Institut an der Freien Universität Berlin, *Rechtswissenschaftliche Abhandlungen*, Band 1 (Berlin Baden-Baden 1974).

Weil, Prosper, 'Principes généraux du droit et contrats d'État' in *Le Droit des Relations Economique Internationales*, Etudes offertes à Berthold Goldman (Paris 1982), p. 387.

Zweigert, Konrad, 'Nichterfüllung auf Grund ausländischer Leistungsverbote', RabelsZ 14 (1942) 283.

A.2.4. Substantive law on state enterprises

Ackermann, Rüdiger, 'Zur wirtschaftlichen Betätigung der öffentlichen Hand: Unzulässige Erweiterung des Warenkatalogs eines Kommunalen Obst- und Gemüsemarktes', *Deutsches Verwaltungsblatt* (1965) 353.

Alfuß, Werner, *Staatliche Haftungsbeschränkung durch Inanspruchnahme privatrechtlicher Organisationsformen*, Diss (Köln 1976). (Function of public enteprises in a modern society especially in the FRG. Legal considerations on state liability for public enterprises. The 'Durchgriffshaftung' of civil law. The law of concerns. State is not considered as an enterprise. State liability according to general clauses of constitutional law. 'Sozial-' und 'Rechtsstaatsprinzip', 'Vertrauensschutzprinzip'.)

Backhaus, Jürgen, *Öffentliche Unternehmen. Zum Wirtschaftsrecht, den Funktionen und Rechtsformen öffentlicher Unternehmen* (2. Auflage, Frankfurt/M. 1980).

Backhaus, Jürgen, Wagner, Richard E., 'Finanzpolitik in der Demokratie' in J. Backhaus, *Offentliche Unternehmen* (2. Auflage, Frankfurt/M. 1980), p. 457.

Badura, Peter, 'Die Erfüllung öffentlicher Aufgaben und die Unternehmenszwecke bei der wirtschaftlichen Betätigung der öffentlichen Hand' in *Staatsrecht-Völkerrecht- Europarecht, Festschrift für H. J. Schlochhauer* (Berlin/New York 1981), p. 3. (The state as entrepreneur – general conditions; state enterprises and market economy; bank and insurance companies controlled by the state; constitutional limits of the activity of state enterprises.)

Barbey, Günther, 'Wahrnehmung staatlicher und gemeindlicher Aufgaben in privatrechtlichen Handlungs- und Entscheidungsformen, Gewerbearchiv' *Beilage Wirtschaft und Verwaltung* (1978), p. 77.

Barten, Ernst-Uwe, 'Die Rechtsstellung des staatlichen Industrieunternehmens in Rumänien, WGO', *Monatsschrift für Ostrecht* 12 (1970) 347.

Bartsch, Günther, 'Zur Wahl der Rechtsform für Unternehmen des privaten Rechts durch die öffentliche Hand', *Der öffentliche Haushalt* 14 (1973) 139.

Batiffol, Henri, 'Arbitration Clauses Concluded Between French Government-Owned Enterprises and Foreign Private Parties', *Columbia Journal of Transnational Law* (1968) 32.

Bettevmann, Karl August, 'Gewerbefreiheit der öffentlichen Hand, Beiträge zu Art. 12 I, 15, 19 III GG' in *Berliner Festschrift für Ernst E. Hirsch* (Berlin 1968), p. 1.

Biermann, Jürgen, *Die Zulässigkeitsvoraussetzungen staatlicher Monopole im Grundgesetz*, Diss. (Mainz 1965).

Bollhauer, Heinz, *Die Rolle der öffentlichen Unternehmen in der sozialen Marktwirtschaft*, Diss. (Marburg 1965).

Brewer-Carias, A. R., *Les Entreprises Publiques en Droit Comparé* (Paris 1968).

Bülck, H., Hämmerlein, H., Jucht, H., Perridon, L., *Verwaltung mit Unternehmen, Politik und Verwaltung*, Heft 10 (Baden-Baden 1968).

Burger, Detlev, *Über die Rechtsstellungen öffentlicher Unternehmen im Privatrechtsverkehr*, Diss. (Tübingen 1966).

'La distinction du droit privé et du droit public et l'enterprise publique'. *Archives de philosophie du droit*, nouvelle série (Paris 1952).

Degenhart, Christl, *Der Durchgriff auf den Staat bei Beteiligung der öffentlichen Hand an Gesellschaften des privaten Rechts*, Diss. (Berlin 1980).

Eckert, Karl Heinz, *Externe Prüfungen staatlicher Beteiligungsunternehmen* (Baden-Baden 1979).

Eichhorn, Peter (ed.), *Auftrag und Führung öffentlicher Unternehmen.* Vorträge und Diskussionsbeiträge der 45. Staatswissenschaftlichen Fortbildungstagung 1977 der Hochschule für Verwaltungswissenschaften Speyer, Schriftenreihe der Hochschule Speyer, Band 68 (Berlin 1977).

Eichhorn, Peter, Rückwardt, Bernd, 'Bibliographie zur öffentlichen Unternehmung 1967 bis 1976' *Zeitschrift für öffentliche und gemeinwirtschaftliche Unternehmen*, Beiheft 1/78.

Fabricant, Robert, 'Developing Country State Enterprises: Performance and Control', 15 *Columbia Journal of Transnational Law*, (1976) 40.

Fischer, Kurt Eduard, 'Das Problem der Rechtsform für öffentliche Unternehmen', *Die öffenliche Wirtschaft* 7 (1958) 2.

Frentzel, Gerhard, *Die gewerbliche Betätigung der öffentlichen Hand.* Ein Problem des Wirtschaftsverfassungsrechts, Schriftenreihe des Deutschen Industrie- und Handelstages, Heft 56 (Bonn 1958).

Frenzke, Dietrich, 'Die Rechtsstellung der sowjetischen Handelsvertretungen nach der Vertragspraxis der UdSSR', *Ost Europa Recht* 9 (1963) 269.

Friedmann, Wolfgang, 'The New Public Corporation and the Law', 10 *Michigan Law Review* (1947) 233.

—— (ed.), *The Public Corporation: A Comparative Symposium* (London 1974).

——, 'Governmental (Public) Enterprises' in *The International Encyclopaedia of Comparative Law*, vol. XIII, Ch. 13 (1972).

——, *Public and Private Enterprise in Mixed Economies* (London 1974).

——, Garner, J. F., *Government Enterprise: A Comparative Study* (New York 1970).

Galbraith, John Kenneth, 'The emerging public corporation' *Business and Society Review* (1972) 54–56.

Haenseler, Hubert, 'Gemeinwirtschaftliche Betrieb und öffentliche Verwaltungen' *Schmalenbachs Zeitschrift für betriebswirtschaftliche Forschung*, Sonderheft 5, (Opladen 1976).

Hettlage, Karl Maria, 'Verfassungsfragen öffentlicher Unternehmen' in *Festschrift für Schmidt-Rimpler* (Bonn 1957), p. 279.

Horak, Hans, *Die wirtschaftliche Betätigung der öffentlichen Hand in der Bundesrepublik Deutschland und ihre Probleme* (Köln und Opladen 1964).

Houin, 'La gestion des entreprises publiques et les méthodes de droit commercial', *Archives de Philosophie du Droit* (1952) 79.

Jakubowski, Jerzy, 'Les entreprises d'état polonaises dans le commerce international (problèmes juridiques)' in *Problemi giuridici dell' impressa, Colloquio promosso dell Academia Nazionale dei Lincei* in collaborazione con l'Universita di Varsavia, Roma, 24–25 nov. 1975, Academia Nazionale dei Lincei (Roma 1976), p. 87. (Organization of state commerce in Poland; applicable law of state enterprises; organization and function of state enterprises in Poland; distinction of legal personality between a state-controlled enterprise and the state; there is not a case of *force majeure* if an act of state hinders the enterprise to perform a contract.)

Janson, Bernd, 'Rechtsformen öffentlicher Unternehmen in der europäischen Gemeinschaft', *Schriften zur öffentlichen Verwaltung und öffentlichen Wirtschaft*, Band 55, (Baden-Baden 1980).

Kaemmerer, Ludwig, 'Die Rechtsnatur der Bundespost' *Deutsches Verwaltungsblatt* (1966) 357 (1st part) and 396 (2nd part).

Kaiser, Joseph H. (ed.), *Planung III. Mittel und Methoden planender Verwaltung* (Baden-Baden 1968).

Karehnke, Helmuth, 'Über Verfassungsfragen zur wirtschaftlichen Betätigung der öffentlichen Hand', 10 *Der öffentliche Haushalt* (1969/70) 233.

——, 'Sollen Beteiligungen des Staates auf Stiftungen des privaten Rechts übergeleitet werden?' *Der öffentliche Haushalt* 13 (1972) 30.

——, 'Die staatliche Betätigung bei Beteiligungsunternehman privaten Rechts und die Prüfung dieser Betätigung *Der öffentliche Haushalt* 15 (1974) 126 (1st part), and 204 (2nd part).

——, 'Die Unternehmen in der Rechtsform einer bundesunmittelbaren juristischen Person des öffentlichen Rechts und ihre Prüfung', *Der öffentliche Haushalt* 16 (1975) 27.

Krüger, Herbert, 'Das Staatsunternehmen – Ort und Rolle in der Marktwirtschaft' *Zeitschrift für Beamtenrecht* (1979) 157.

Kull, Edgar, *Privatrecht als Mittel der Verwaltung. Studien zur Vertauschbarkeit öffentlichen und privaten Rechts*, Diss. (Heidelberg 1967).

Langrod, Georges, 'L'entreprise public en droit administratif comparé', 8 *Revue droit international droit comparé* (1956) 213.

Law and Public Enterprise in Asia. Praeger special studies in international economics and development. Based on a colloquium held in Sri Lanka, May 1974 (New York 1976).

Mestre, Achille, 'Les Etablissements Publics Industriels et Commerciaux et le recours à l'arbitrage (L'apport de l'art. 7 de la loi 75-596 du 9 Juillet 1975)' *Revue de l'Arbitrage* (1976) 3.

Mielke, Jürgen, *Die Abgrenzung der juristischen Person des öffentlichen Rechts von der juristischen Person des Privatrechts*, Diss. (Hamburg 1965).

Momberger, Eckhard, *Bundesunternehmen im Wettbewerb mit der privaten Wirtschaft*, Diss. (Marburg 1968).

Münch, Paul, 'Rechtsformen kommunaler Unternehmen' in *Öffentliche Wirtschaft und Gemeinwirtschaft* (1978), p. 108.

Oettle, Karl, 'Grundlagen öffentlicher Betriebe. Ausgewählte Aufsätze zur Zielsetzung, Führung, Organisation, Finanzierung und Rechnung öffentlicher Betriebe', Schriften zur öffentlichen Verwaltung und öffentlichen Wirtschaft, Nr. 14, (Baden-Baden 1976).

Pavel, Uwe, *Eignet sich die Stiftung für den Betrieb erwerbswirtschaftlicher Unternehmen?* (Bad Homburg 1976).

Plöchl, Gerhard, *Vereine als öffentliche Unternehmen* (Wien . . . 1972).

Pretnar, Stojan, 'Das Unternehmen in Jugoslawien und seine Rechtsstellung' *Ost-Europa-Recht* 7 (1961) 233.

Püttner, Günter, *Die öffentlichen Unternehmen.* Verfassungsfragen zur wirtschaftlichen Betätigung der öffentlichen Hand. (Bad Homburg 1969).
——, 'Rechtsformen im Überblick', Die positiven und negativen Folgen einzelner Rechtsformen der öffentlichen Unternehmen müssen systematisch erfaßt werden. *Die öffentliche Wirtschaft und Gemeinwirtschaft* (1977), p. 101.
Ress, Georg, 'Regierungskontrolle von öffentlichen (staatlichen und halbstaatlichen) Industrieunternehmen' in *Liber Amicorum Aubin*, hrsg. von F.-W. Baer-Kaupert u. a., Kehl am Rhein (Strasbourg 1979), p. 129.
Ritschl, Hans, 'Offentliche Unternehmen' in *Handwörterbuch der Sozialwissenschaften,* Band 10, 1959, p. 516.
Rubin (ed.), *Foreign Development Lending – Legal Aspects* (1971).
Savy, Robert, *L'intervention des pouvoirs publics dans la vie économique.* Etude de droit comparé. Tôme 1: Institutions et politiques, par R. Savy et M. Fromant. Presses universitaires de France. Publications de la Faculté de droit et des sciences économiques de Limoges.
Schmidt-Salzer, Joachim, 'Tätigwerden des Staates in zivilrechtlichen Handlungsformen im Bereich der Daseinsvorsorge und des Beschaffungswesens', *Wirtschaftsrecht* 1 (1972) 103.
Schütz, Eberhard, *Die Rechtsstellung des staatlichen Industrieunternehmens*. Ostrechtliche Schriften der Abteilung für Ostrechtsforschung im Seminar für deutsches und nordisches Recht der Universität Hamburg (Hamburg 1968).
Shepard, P., *Sovereignty and State-Owned Commercial Entities* (New York 1951).
Starr, Robert, *East-West Business Transactions* (New York/Washington/London 1974).
Surbiguet, Marcel, *Les sociétés d'économie mixte dans les pays en voie de développement*. A partir de l'exemple Malgache. Bibliotheque de droit international, tôme LIV, 2 volumes (Paris 1970). (A general survey over function and organization of mixed enterprises; comparative study of French and Madagascan law; analysis of the statutes of several Madagascan mixed enterprises; urgan and industrial texts and statistics (vol. 2).)
Tosato, Gianluigi, 'Some considerations on the legal structure of public and private multinational enterprises' *Italian Yearbook of International Law* (1976) 122. (Structure of multinational enterprises with special reference to public state-created enterprises).
Triebenstein, Olaf, *Die industriellen Staatsunternehmen und die Möglichkeit und Notwendigkeit ihrer instrumentalen Verwendung in marktwirtschaftlich organisierten Volkswirtschaften*, Diss. (Berlin 1958).
Verdera y Tuells, Evelio (ed.), *La Empresa Publica, Studia Albornotiana* vol. X, two volumes (Zaragoza 1970). (General part: the function and organization of the public enterprise in a mixed economy; special part: comparative aspects of the problem; the system of public enterprises in several countries in East and West.)
Virole, Jean, 'Réflexions sur l'application d'un droit de groupes de sociétés aux entreprises publiques', 26 *Revue trimestriele du droit roumain* (1973) 177.
Vogel, Klaus, 'Die wirtschaftliche Betätigung öffentlicher Verwaltungsträger in Handel und Industrie und ihre rechtliche Regelung' in E. v. Caemmerer/K. Zweigert (ed.), *Deutsche Landesreferate zum VII Internationalen Kongreß dür Rechtsvergleichung in Uppsala* (1966) (Berlin/Tübingen 1967), pp. 461–477.
Wenger, Karl, *Die öffentliche Unternehmung*. Ein Beitrag zur Lehre der Wirtschaftsverwaltung und zur Theorie des Wirtschaftsverwaltungsrechts (Wien . . . 1969).
Witte, Eberhard, Hauschild, Jürgen, *Die öffentliche Unternehmung im Interessenkonflikt* (Berlin 1966).
Zagaris, Bruce, 'The rising utility of the public international corporation', 6 *Denver Journal of International Law and Politics* 43.

A.2.5. Law of arbitration

Batiffol, Henri, 'Arbitration Clauses Concluded between French Government-Owned Enterprises and Foreign Private Parties', 7 *Columbia Journal of Transnational Law* (1968) 32.
Bauer, 'Die Bedeutung des Europäischen Übereinkommens über die internationale Handelsschiedsgerichtsbarkeit für den Handel mit Ostblockstaaten', 14 *Recht in Ost und West* (1970) 61.
Böckstiegel, Karl-Heinz, 'The Relationship between the UNCITRAL Arbitration Rules and the National Law Applicable to the Arbitration', Published in German version RIW (1982) 706.

——, 'Die UNCITRAL-Verfahrensordnung für Wirtschaftsgerichtsbarkeit und das anwendbare nationale Recht' RIW (1982) 706.

—— (ed), *Vertragspraxis und Streiterledigung im Wirtschaftsverkehr mit arabischen Staaten*, Schriftenreihe des Deutschen Instituts für Schiedsgerichtswesen, Band 2 (Köln/Berlin/Bonn/München 1981).

Frenzke, Dietrich, 'Prozessuale Immunitäten der sowjetischen Handelsvertretungen nach den zwischenstaatlichen Verträgen', 10 *Ost Europa Recht* (1964) 237.

Gause, Hermann, Melsheimer, Klaus, 'Beiträge zum sowjetischen Außenhandelsrecht'. Berichte des Osteuropa-Instituts an der Freien Universität Berlin – Reihe *Wirtschaft und Recht*, Heft 63 (Berlin 1964).

Jakubowski, J., 'The Settlement of Foreign Trade Disputes in Poland', 11 *International & Comparative Law Quarterly* (1962) 806. (Organization of foreign trade arbitration in Poland; applicable law; rules of procedure; discussion of several cases.)

Knapp, 'The Function, Organization and Activities of Foreign Trade Corporations in the European Socialist Countries' in Schmitthoff (ed.), *The Sources of the Law of International Trade* (London 1964), p. 52.

Pisar, S., 'The Communist System of Foreign-Trade Adjudication', 72 *Harvard Law Review* (1959) 1409.

Ribolzi, C., 'The Choice and Appointment of Board of Arbitrators in Disputes Concerning Public Works in Local Public Bodies' in *Commercial Arbitration, Essays in Memoriam Eugenio Minoli* (Turin 1974), p. 425.

Rithman, Zvone, 'Arbitration between Governments and Government Controlled Bodies and Foreign Business Firms', *Jugoslavenska Revija Za Medunarodno Pravo III* (1960) 324. (Under Yugoslav law the state may on its own behalf and on behalf of its agencies conclude agreements on arbitration. There are no 'state controlled enterprises' in Yugoslavia since all enterprises are owned and controlled by their bodies of management and representatives. They can't claim sovereign immunity.)

Trammer, Henryk, 'La Convention de Moscou sur l'arbitrage du 26 mai 1972', in *Commercial Arbitration, Essays in Memoriam Eugenio Minoli* (Turin 1974), p. 517.

A.2.6. Relevance of being a separate legal entity

Batiffol, Henri, 'Arbitration Clauses Concluded between French Government-Owned Enterprises and Foreign Private Parties', 7 *Columbia Journal of Transnational Law* (1968) 32.

Bernstein, Herbert, 'Durchgriff bei juristischen Personen, insbesondere Gesellschaften in Staatshand. Kollisionsrechtliche und neuere materiellrechtliche Erkenntnisse im Rückblick auf den chilenischen Kupferstreit' in *Festschrift für K. Zweigert*, p. 37. (Development of the theory of 'piercing the corporate veil'; German considerations; special groups of cases; law applicable in such cases; survey over German practice and theory; protection of creditors; outweigh of interests; application of the *lex causae*.)

Böckstiegel, Karl-Heinz, 'Der Staat als Vertragspartner ausländischer Privatunternehmen', *Völkerrecht und Internationales Wirtschaftsrecht*, Band 1 (Frankfurt/M. 1971).

——, *Der Durchgriff auf den Staat.* Thesen zur funktionellen Identifizierung staatlichen Handelns (Frankfurt/M. 1972). ('Piercing the corporate veil' of state enterprises; identification of such enterprises with the state; functional definition of state activity; groups of cases 'piercing the veil' in internal law; state and foreign enterprises; group of cases for an international 'piercing the veil' doctrine.)

Bratus, S. K., *Subjects of civil law*, U.S.S.R., State Publishing House of Juridical Literature (1950).

Burkhard, *Neuere Probleme des Haftungsdurchgriffs bei juristischen Personen im Recht der Vereinigten Staaten von Amerika* (Heidelberg 1969).

Carabiber, Charles, 'L'arbitrage internationale et le problème de l'immunité de juridiction des états et des collectivités publiques signataires d'une clause compromissoire insérée dans un contrat de droit privé', *Revue de l'Arbitrage* (1967) 49.

Domke, Martin, 'Government Immunity in Foreign Trade Arbitration: A Comparative Survey of the Recent Practice' in *Hommages F. Eisemann*, p. 45. (The meaning of sovereign immunity and the development of the doctrine; distinction between sovereign and commercial activities of the state according to international law or national legislation; practical problems: international investment, expropriation and maritime transactions.)

Drobnig, Ulrich, *Haftungsdurchgriff bei Kapitalgesellschaften, Arbeiten zur Rechtsvergleichung*, Heft 4 (Frankfurt/M./Berlin 1959).

Hervey, 'The Immunity of Foreign States When Engaged in Commercial Enterprises: A Proposed Solution', 27 *Michigan Law Review* (1929) 751.

Homburger, 'Zum Durchgriff im schweizerischen Gesellschaftsrecht', SJZ 67 (1971) 249.

Jakubowski, Jerzy, 'Les entreprises d'état polonaises dans le commerce international (problèmes juridiques)' in *Problemi giuridici dell' impressa*, Colloquio promosso dell' Academia Nazionale dei Lincei in collaborazione con l'Universita di Varsavia, Roma, 24–25 nov. 1975, (Academia Nazionale dei Lincei, Roma, 1976), p. 87.

Khadjavi-Gontard, Bardia, Hausmann, Rainer, 'Zurechenbarkeit von Hoheitsakten und subsidiäre Staatshaftung bei Verträgen mit ausländischen Staatsunternehmen', *Recht der Internationalen Wirtschaft/Außenwirtschaftsdienst des Betriebsberaters* (1980), p. 533.

——, 'Haftungsdurchgriff auf ausländische Staaten', RIW (1983) 1.

Lalive, Pierre, 'Arbitrage international et ordre public suisse. Une surprenante décision du Tribunal féderal: l'arret *SGTM/Bangladesh*', *Zeitschrift für schweizerisches Recht*, 97 neue Folge (1978) I, 529. (Dissolution of a state enterprise in order to escape arbitration.)

Madl, 'State in the Economy and Problems of State Immunity with Special Regard to Economic Integration' in *Gedächtnisschrift für Albert Ehrenzweig* (1976), p. 89.

Naendrup, P. H., *Privatrechtliche Haftungsbeschränkung und staatliche Verantwortung*. Zur Organisationsfreiheit von Staatspersonen in handelsrechtlichen Formen (Bielefeld 1967).

Note (St. G. Nagle), 'Sovereign immunity: *Trendtex Trading Corporation* v. *Central Bank of Nigeria*' [1977] 2 WLR 356 (CA), 13 *Texas International Law Journal* 131.

Note (Michael T. Janik), 'International Law – Labour Law – NLRB Jurisdiction over Foreign Sovereigns Operating within the United States: State Bank of India' 12 *Journal of International Law & Economics* (1978) 459.

Pisar, Samuel, *Praxis des Osthandels*. Übersetzung und Bearbeitung Dr. Karl Lang (Frankfurt/M. 1973).

Przetacznik, Franciszek, 'The Sovereign Immunity of Foreign States and International Commercial Arbitration', *Revue de droit international de sciences diplomatiques et politiques* (1979) 188 (no. 3) and 291 (no. 4).

Raupach, A., *Der Durchgriff im Steuerrecht*. Zugleich ein Beitrag zum Verhältnis des Deutschen und Internationalen Steuerrechts zum Zivil-, Verfassungs- und Völkerrecht (München 1968).

Recent Development (T. A. Peterson/H. W. Hoyt), 'Foreign Sovereign Immunity', 9 *Georgia Journal of International and Comparative Law* (1979) 111.

Recent Development (C. G. O.), 'Labor: State Bank of India, 229 N.(ational) L.(abor) R.(elation) B.(oard) 137 95 L.R.R.M. (1977), 1141; 13 *Texas International Law Journal* (1977) 146.

Recent Development (D. N.), 'Admiralty: *Compania National de Navegacion, SA* 1977 AMC. 1135 CDC Canal Zone 1977', 13 *Texas International Law Journal* (1978) 378.

Ress, Georg, 'Regierungskontrolle von öffentlichen (staatlichen und halbstaatlichen) Industrieunternehmen' in *Festschrift für B. C. H. Aubin, Kehl am Rhein* (Strasbourg 1979), p. 129. (Governmental control over state or semi-state enterprises in German and European law.)

Schmitthoff, Clive M., 'The Claim of Sovereign Immunity in the Law of International Trade', 7 *International & Comparative Law Quarterly* (1958) 452. (Sovereign immunity in international trade; theories of immunity; immunity of state-owned corporations; criterion for granting immunity; intention of the sovereign to act on the level of private law.)

——, 'Corporate Existence' in *Palmer's Company Law* (London 1976), Chapter 18.

Seidl-Hohenveldern, Ignaz, 'Besitzen Staatsbetriebe und ihr Staat gleiche oder verschiedene Rechtspersönlichkeiten?', *Recht in Ost und West* 10 (1966) 1. ('State enterprise' is not to be identified with the state; the impact of 'state enterprises' in economic relationship between states; 'Hoheitsakte' of 'state enterprises'.)

——, 'Neue Entwicklungen im Recht der Staatenimmunität' in *Festschrift für G. Beitzke* (Berlin/New York 1979), p. 1081.

Serick, Rolf, *Rechtsform und Realität juristischer Personen* (Tübingen 1955).

Setser, 'The Immunity Waiver of State-Controlled Business Enterprises in United States Commercial Treaties', *Proceedings of American Society of International Law* (1961) 89.

Singer, Michael, 'The Act of State Doctrine of the United Kingdom: An Analysis with Comparison to United States Practice', 75 *American Journal of International Law* (1981) 283.

Thompson, Jere Geiger, 'Foreign Sovereign Immunity – The Status of Legal Entities in Socialist Countries as Defendants under the Foreign Sovereign Immunities Act of 1976', 12 *The Vanderbilt Journal of Transnational Law* (Winter 1979) 165.

Trammer, H., 'L'organisation juridique du commerce exterieur polonais en géneral et l'organisation de ses institutions executives en particulier' in *Aspects juridiques du commerce avec les pays d'économie planifiée* (Paris 1961), p. 212.

Wengler, Wilhelm, 'Nouveaux aspects de la problematique des contrats entre état et personnes privées', XIV *Revue belge de droit international* (1978–79) 415.

Wilser, H., *Der Durchgriff bei Kapitalgesellschaften im Steuerrecht* (Heidelberg 1960).

Wormser, Maurice, 'Piercing the Veil of Corporate Entity', *Columbia Law Review* (1912) 496

Zlatesku, Victor Dan, 'The self-managing economic unit not having legal personality and the capacity of subject of civil law', 24 *Revue roumaine des sciences sociales – série des sciences juridiques* (1980) 205.

A.2.7. Enforcement of arbitration awards against state enterprises*

Böckstiegel, Karl-Heinz (ed.), *Vertragspraxis und Streiterledigung im Wirtschaftsverkehr mit arabischen Staaten*, Schriftenreihe des Deutschen Instituts für Schiedsgerichtswesen, Band 2 (Köln/Berlin/Bonn/München 1981).

Capatina, Octavian, Ianculescu, Dinn, 'La solution des questions de compétence internationale en instance d'exequatur', 24 *Revue roumaine des sciences sociales – série des sciences juridiques* (1980) 215.

Cappelli-Perciballi, Lionello, 'The Application of the New York Convention of 1958 to Disputes Between States and Between State Entities and Private Individuals: The Problem of Sovereign Immunity', 12 *International Lawyer* (1978) 197.

Carabiber, Charles, 'L'immunité de juridiction et d'exécution des états collectivités et établissements publics au regard de l'obligation assumée par une clause compromissoire insérée dans les contrats internationaux de droit privé' in *International Arbitration – Liber Amicorum for Martin Domke* (The Hague 1967), p. 23.

Gilbert, Peter, 'A symposium of the enforcement of foreign judgements and arbitral awards', 17 *Vanderbilt Journal of International Law* 359.

L'immunité de juridication et d'exécution des Etats. A propos du projet de Convention du Conseil de l'Europe, Actes du Colloque conjoint des 30 et 31 janvier 1969, Centre de droit international de l'institut de Sociologie de l'Université de Louvain, vol. 4, (Brussels 1969).

Jakubowski, Jerzy, 'The Recognition and Enforcement of Foreign Arbitration Awards in Poland', VII *Polish Yearbook of International Law* (1975) 65.

Junker, Joel R., 'The Public Policy Defense to Recognition and Enforcement of Foreign Arbitral Awards', 7 *California Western International Law Journal* (1977) 228. (Discussion of several cases on arbitration and public policy in the United States. General considerations not only especially to state enterprises.)

Lalive, Jean Flavien, 'Swiss Law and Practice in Relations to Measures of Execution against the Property of a Foreign State' in X *Netherlands YIL* (1979), p. 153.

Ohmstead, 'The Enforcement of Arbitral Awards against a Foreign Government', lecture before the German American Lawyers Association, Düsseldorf, May 9, 1983 (not yet published).

Orban, Frank A., 'The Challenge To The Enforcement Of Socialist Arbitral Awards', 17 *Virginia Journal of International Law* (1977) 375.

Seidl-Hohenveldern, Ignaz, 'State Immunity: Federal Republic of Germany' in X *Netherlands YIL* (1979), p. 55.

Schachter, Oskar, 'Enforcement of International Judicial and Arbitral Decisions', 54 *American Journal of International Law* (1960) 1.

* Till now there are no cases of enforcement against enterprises of CMEA countries because they fulfil the awards made against them voluntarily, comp. *Stalev*, Practical Application in the Field of Arbitration in Private Exchanges between East and West, Contribution in the International Meeting on Arbitration, Como, May 21–22, 1981 (unpublished, available at the Cologne University Chair of International Business Law).

Strohbach, Heinz, *Anerkennung und Vollstreckung schiedsgerichtlicher Entscheidungen in der DDR*, Kammer für Außenhandel der DDR, (East Berlin).

Tsegah, Francis A., Tiewul, S. Azadon, 'Arbitration and the Settlement of Commercial Disputes: A Selective Survey of African Practice', 9 *Journal of World Trade Law* (1975) 378. (Contracts with African governments; enforcements of arbitration awards.)

Waehler, Jan-Peter, 'Die Außenhandels- und See- Schiedsgerichtsbarkeit in der UdSSR.' Institutionen, Verfahren und Ermittlung des anwendbaren Rechts, Osteuropa-Institut an der Freien Universität Berlin, *Rechtswissenschaftliche Abhandlungen*, Band 1 (Berlin, Baden-Baden 1974).

West, Luther, 'Award Enforcement Provisions of the World Bank Convention', 23 *Arbitration Journal* (1968) 38.

A.2.8. Suggestions for improvements in international business law and practice

Stalev, Zhivko, 'Practical Applications in the Field of Arbitration in Private Exchanges between East and West', Relation in the International Meeting on Arbitration, Como 21/22 may 1981 (unpublished available at the Cologne University Chair of International Business Law).

A.3. REPORTS AND COMMENTS ON SPECIFIC NATIONAL OR REGIONAL LEGAL SYSTEMS

Argentina

Elverdin, Jose Pablo, 'Arbitration Clauses in Contracts between Argentine Governmental Bodies and Private Parties: Evolution of the Argentine Law and New Developments in International Law and Regional Economic Arrangements' (unpublished available at the Cologne University Chair of International Business Law).

Naón, Grigera, Samtleben, Jürgen, 'Schiedsgerichtsbarkeit in Argentinien', RIW/AWD (1983) 721.

Asia

Law and Public Enterprise in Asia (New York 1976).

Belgium

De Page, Van de Walle, De Ghelcke, 'Les personnes morales étrangères et l'ordre publique international belge', *Revue pratique des sociétés civiles et commerciales* (1979) 1.

Dermine, Louis, *L'Arbitrage commercial en Belgique* (Brussels 1975).

Fettweis, Albert, Arets, Jean, 'L'arbitrage entre gouvernements ou personnes de droit public et personnes de droit privé', *Revue de l'Arbitrage* (1961) 154. (A national Belgian survey.)

——, 'L'arbitrage entre gouvernements ou personnes de droit public et personnes de droit privé', 6 *Annales de la Faculté de Droit de Liège* (1961) 339. (Belgian practice on the subject.)

Rivero, Jean, 'Personnes morals de droit public et arbitrage', *Revue de l'Arbitrage* (1973) 263. (Survey of French and Belgian practice and legislation.)

Stassen, Jacques, 'Le role du Comité Supérieur de Controle et l'Arbitrage des conflits entre l'Etat et ses fournisseurs', 6 *Annales de la Faculté de Droit de Liège*, (1961) 379 esp. pp. 405–417. (Belgian practice and comparative survey; suggestions for a legislative intervention.)

Canada

Kos-Rabcewicz-Zubkowski, L., *Commercial and Civil Law Arbitration in Canada* (University of Ottawa Press 1978).

Lamont, Douglas, 'Emerging Neo-Mercantilism in Canadian Policy Toward State Enterprises and Foreign Direct Investment', 8 *Vanderbilt Journal of Transnational Law* (Fall 1974) 121. (Developments in Canadian policy toward its relationships with the USA; mercantilistic trends; creation of state enterprises; function and aims of these enterprises; legal forms.)

China

Hsu, S. P., 'The Enforcement of American Arbitral Awards in the Republic of China', *Annals of the Chinese Society of International Law* 51 (1969).

Council of Mutual Economic Aid

Böckstiegel, K.-H., Glossner, O., *Internationale Schiedsgerichtsbarkeit im Ost-West Handel* (Baden-Baden 1975).

Capatina, Octave, 'L'arbitrage du commerce extérieur selon la convention de Moscou de 1972', *Journal de Droit International* (*Clunet*) (1975) 503.

Cornil, Henri, 'Deux instruments pour l'arbitrage commercial international entre parties de l'Est et de l'Ouest de l'Europe', 1 *Droit et pratique du commerce international* (1975) 475.

Fink, Karl Hermann, 'L'arbitrage socialiste dans le commerce Est-Ouest', 1 *Droit et pratique du commerce international* (1975) 367.

Kos-Rabcewicz-Zubkowski, Ludwik, *East-European Rules on the Validity of International Arbitration Agreements* (Manchester/New York 1970).

Pfaff, Dieter, 'Vereinheitlichung der Außenhandels-Arbitrage der RGW – Länder und ihre Auswirkungen auf die internationale Handelsschiedsgerichtsbarkeit im Ost-West-Handel, Recht der Internationalen', *Wirtschaft/Außenwirtschaftsdienst des Betriebsberaters* (1976), p. 253.

Rajski, Jerzy, 'Basic Principles of International Trade Law and Certain European Socialist States and of East-West Trade Relations', 4 *Droit et pratique du commerce international* (1978) 9.

Sarközy, T., 'Bericht über das Gesetz der staatlichen Unternehmen, bzw, über die Änderungen in der rechtlichen Regelung der juristischen Personen im Zusammenhang mit dem Zivilgesetzbuch' *Acta juridica* (1978) 422.

Stalev, V. J., 'L'arbitrage économique internationale dans les pays-membres du CAEM après la Convention de Moscou de 1972' in *Problèmes juridiques de l'integration économique socialiste* (Sofia 1977).

Strohbach, Heinz, 'Wesenszüge und Besonderheiten der Schiedsgerichtsbarkeit in den Mitgliedsländern des RGW', in W. Seiffert (ed.), *Sozialistische ökonomische Integration, Rechtsfragen* (East Berlin 1974), p. 181.

Supramovitz, Stefan, 'The Law of State Owned Enterprises in a Socialist State', 26 *Law & Contemporary Problems* (1961) 734.

Ustor, Endre, 'Arbitration in CMEA Member Countries' in 14 *Communicazioni e studi*, vol. 14 (1975): Il processo internazionale. Studi in onore di Gaetano Morelli, p. 957.

Eire – Ireland

Golding, G. M., *The Juristic Basis of the Irish State Enterprise.*

Federal Republic of Germany

Albert, Michael, 'Arrestverfahren gegen ausländische staatliche Unternehmen am Vermögensgerichtsstand', IPRax (1983) 55.

Backhaus, Jürgen, *Öffentliche Unternehmen – Zum Wirtschaftsrecht, den Funktionen und Rechtsformen öffentlicher Unternehmen*. (Frankfurt/Main, 1977).

Böckstiegel, Karl-Heinz, *Der Durchgriff auf den Staat* (Frankfurt/Main, 1972).

——, 'Internationale Schiedsgerichtsbarkeit zwischen Staaten und Privatunternehmen' in *Außenwirtschaftsdienst des Betriebs-Beraters* (1965) 101.

——, *Der Staat als Vertragspartner ausländischer Privatunternehmen* (Frankfurt/Main 1971).

——, 'Besondere Probleme der Schiedsgerichtsbarkeit zwischen Privatunternehmen und ausländischen Staaten oder Staatsunternehmen' *Neue Juristische Wochenschrift* (1957) 1577.

Borchers, K. G., *Verträge von Staaten mit ausländischen Privatpersonen* (Göttingen 1966).

Emmerich, Volker, *Das Wirtschaftsrecht der öffentlichen Unternehmen* (Bad Homburg v.d.H/Berlin/Zürich 1969).

Hübner, Ulrich, 'Der Durchgriff bei juristischen Personen im europäischen Gesellschafts- und Unternehmensrecht' *Juristen Zeitung* (1978) 703.

Junker, H., *Charakterisierung und rechtliche Umgrenzung der öffentlich-wirtschaftlichen Unternehmertätigkeit*, Dissertation (Göttingen 1965).

Püttner, Günter, *Die öffentlichen Unternehmen*. Verfassungsfragen zur wirtschaftlichen Betätigung der öffentlichen Hand, (Bad Homburg 1969).

Schlosser, Peter, 'Schiedsgerichtsbarkeit und öffentlichrechtlich beeinflußte Streitgegenstände' in *Festschrift für Arthur Bülow* (München 1981) p. 189.

Stoll, Jutta, *Vereinbarungen zwischen Staat und ausländischem Investor* (Berlin 1982).

——, 'Rechtsnatur und Bestandsschutz von Vereinbarungen zwischen Staaten und ausländischen privaten Investoren' *Recht der internationalen Wirtschaft* (1981) 808.

Finland

Modeen, Tore, 'Regimen de las actividades comerciales et industriales de los poderes publicos en Finlandia', 3 *Annales de l'Université de Carabobo* (1970), 329.

France

Barckhausen, 'Etudes sur la théorie des domaines publics' 18 *Revue du droit public* (1902) 401.
Becher, Gerd Wilfried, *Die Rechtsstellung verstaatlichter Wirtschaftsunternehmen in Frankreich*. Diss. (Köln 1967).
Carabiber, Ch., 'Chronique sur un arret' *Revue de l'Arbitrage* (1966) 93. (Remarks on the *Galakis* case).
——, Troisième Colloque des Facultés du Droit. *Le fonctionnement des entreprises nationalisées en France* (Paris 1956).
Connois, René, *La notion d'établissement public en droit administratif français* (Paris 1959).
Delion, André, *L'état et les entreprises publiques* (1958).
——, 'La distinction du droit privé et du droit public et l'entreprise publique', *Archives de philosophie du droit*, nouvelle série (Paris 1952).
Ducouloux, Claude, *Les sociétés d'économie mixte en France et en Italie* (Paris 1963).
Gaudernet, Paul Marie, 'Le controle financier des entreprises publiques', 88 *Revue de droit public* (1972) 293.
Goufreville, Max, 'L'evolution de la jurisprudence francaise en matière d'arbitrage et les projets de réforme' *Revue de l'Arbitrage* (1966) 55.
Groupe de travail du comité-interministeriel des entreprises publiques (Président: S. Nora), *Rapport sur les entreprises publiques* (Paris 1967).
Hanson, A. H., 'Organisation des entreprises d'état', 31 *Revue internationale des sciences administratives* (1965) 107.
Mazeaud/Vedel, 'EDF et GDR ont-ils le capacité de compromettre?' *Cahiers de documentation juridique des EDF et GDF* (1950) 224.
Mestre, Achille, 'Les Etablissements Publics Industriels et Commerciaux et le recours à l'arbitrage (L'apport de l'art. 7 de la loi 75-596 du 9 juillet 1975)', *Revue de l'Arbitrage* (1976) 3.
Motulsky, Henri, 'L'arbitrage commercial et les personnes morales de droit public', *Revue de l'Arbitrage* (1956) 38.
——, 'La capacité de compromettre des Etablissements publics à caractère commercial (A propos l'arret "Société Nationale de Vente des Surplus")', *Revue de l'Arbitrage* (1958) 39.
Rivero, Jean, 'Personnes Morals de droit public et arbitrage', *Revue de l'Arbitrage* (1973) 263. (Survey of French and Belgian practice and legislation.)

German Democratic Republic

'Aus der Spruchpraxis des Schiedsgerichts bei der Kammer für Außenhandel der DDR (Allgemeine Lieferbedingungen des RGW)', *Recht im Außenhandel* (1979) No. 40, pp. 13–15.
Andrae, Peter (ed.), Aus der Spruchpraxis des Schiedsgerichts bei Kammer für Außenhandel der DDR 1954–1968 und 1969–1976. Kammer für Außenhandel der DDR (Berlin 1979).
Geske, Otto Erich, *Die staatlichen juristischen Personen sowjetzonalen Rechts*. Eine Untersuchung der Rechtsstruktur der volkseigenen Industriebetriebe. Diss. (Göttingen 1959).
Haendcke-Hoppe, Maria, Mampel, Siegfried 'Die Schiedsgerichtsbarkeit im Außenhandel der DDR', *Recht in Ost und West* (1976) 75.
Strohbach, Heinz, Völter, Jochen, 'Die neuen Rechtsgrundlagen der sozialistischen Außenhandelsschiedsgerichtsbarkeit', *Recht im Außenhandel* (1976) 1.

Hungary

Sebestyen, 'Lizenzverkehr mit Ungarn, Referat anläßlich der ungarischen Wirtschaftslage in Düsseldorf 1970', Reported by Stumpf/Lindstaedt, *Außenwirtschaftsdienst* (1972) 228, n. 17.

Indonesia

Fabricant, Robert, 'Production Sharing Contracts in the Indonesian Petroleum Industry' 16 *Harvard International Law Journal* (1975) 302.

Iran

Böckstiegel, Karl-Heinz, 'Schwierigkeiten bei Gerichtsstansvereinbarungen und Schiedsklauseln im Wirtschaftsverkehr mit dem Iran', *Außenwirtschaftdienst im Betriebsberater* (1974) 117.

Israel

'Government Corporations Law, 5735 – 1975' in: *Sefer Ha Chukkim* No. 770, 4.7.1975. Published with authorized translation in English: *Laws of the State of Israel*, vol. 29 (5735- 1974/75), p. 162.

Italy

Calgano, Francesco, 'La societa per azioni in mano publica', 3 *Politica dei Diritto* (1972) 681.

Gajl, Natalie, 'Les entreprises d'état en France, en Italie et en Pologne: Quelques aspects juridiques', 27 *Revue internationale des sciences administratives* (1961) 154.

Holland, Stuart (ed.), *The State as Entrepreneur: New Dimensions for Public Enterprise: The IRI-State-Shareholding Formula* (London 1972).

Posner, M. V., Woolf, S. J., *Italian Public Enterprise* (Cambridge (Mass.) 1967).

Seraceno, Pasquale, 'The Italian System of State-Held Enterprises', 11 *Journal of International Law & Economics* (1977) 407.

Latin America

Dickey, Walter, Book Review for *Legal Choices for Enterprises in the Third World* by Robert C. Pozen (New York 1976): 52 *New York University Law Review* (1977) 205.

Ibarra Escamilla, Juan Luis, *Régimen de la participacion estadal en las industrias basicas o estratégicas, Mercado comun centroamericano*, Guatemala (1973), p. 149.

Instituto para la Integracion de America Latina, 'Estudio sobre el régimen legal de las empresas públicas latinoamericanas y su accion internacional', 6 *Derecho de la Integracion* (1973) 149.

Kaplan, Marcos, 'Intervención del estado y empresa publica en la America Latin contemporanea: Los aspectos politicos e institucionales', *Revista de estudios politicos* (1978) 5.

Pozen, Robert C., *Legal Choices for State Enterprises in the Third World* (New York 1976).

Less Developed Countries

'La distinction du droit privé et du droit public et l'entreprise publique', *Archives de philosophie du droit*, nouvelle série (Paris 1952).

Bencheneb, Ali, 'La conclusion des marchés en Algérie', *Droit et pratique du commerce international* (1982) 549.

Fabricant, Robert, 'Developing Country State Enterprises Performance and Control', 15 *Columbia Journal of Transnational Law* (1976) 40.

Mascaranhas, R. C., 'A System's View of the Measurement of the Performance of Public Enterprise in India', 5 *Policy Science* (1974) 29.

Pozen, Robert C., *Legal Choices for State Enterprises in the Third World* (New York 1976).

Libya

Alem, Mustafa El, 'L'arbitrage dans les litiges relatifs aux contrats administratifs libyens', *Revue de l'Arbitrage* (1983) No. 3, 295.

von Mehren, Robert B.,/Kourides, P. Nicholas, 'International Arbitration between States and Foreign Private Parties: The Libyan Nationalization Cases', 75 *American Journal of International Law*, (July 1981) 476.

Poland

Böckstiegel, Karl-Heinz, 'Schiedsgerichtsbarkeit als Entscheidungsinstanz in deutsch-polnischen Wirtschaftsbeziehungen' in Drittes deutsch-polnisches Juristen-Kolloquium, Band 3 *Wirtschaftsbeziehungen* (Baden-Baden 1977) p. 93.

Frendl, Ludwig, 'Die sozialistischen juristischen Personen und die Rechtsnatur ihrer gegenseitigen Verträge im polnischen ZGB', *Recht in Ost und West* (1970) 56.
Gola, Alfred, 'Die Außenhandelsschiedsgerichtsbarkeit in Polen' *Zeitschrift für Rechtsvergleichung* 19 (1978) 18.
Jakubowski, Jerzy, 'The Recognition and Enforcement of Foreign Arbitral Awards in Poland' VII *Polish Yearbook of International Law*, (1975), p. 65.
——, *The Problem of Immunity of State Enterprises* (Studia Prwanicze 1967).
——, 'Les Entreprises d'Etat Polonaise dans le Commerce International (Problèmes juridique)' in *Colloquio premosso dall'Academia Nazionalle dei Cincei* in Collaborazione con l'Universita di Varsavia, Roma 24–25 novembre 1975 (Rome 1976).
Aus der Spruchpraxis des Internationalen Schiedsgerichts für die See- und Binnenschiffahrt in Gdynia, Kammer für Außenhandel der Deutschen Demokratischen Republik, Volume II (Berlin East, 1979).
Sadowska, Eva, 'Origins of Creation of International Socialist Enterprises', 8 *Studies on international relations* (1977) 147.
Wengerek, Edmund, 'Das Verhältnis von staatlicher Arbitrage und Zivilverfahren in Polen', RabelsZ 42 (1978), 550. (Approximation of state arbitration procedure to the procedure in the civil court; the matter in controversy rather than the deciding organ determines the nature of the procedure.)

Rumania

Barten, Ernst- Uwe, 'Die Rechtsstellung des staatlichen Industrieunternehmens in Rumänien, WGO' *Monatsschrift für Ostrecht* 12 (1970) 347.
Capatina, Octavian, Zilberstein, Savelly, 'La reconnaissance et l'exécution des décisions judiciaires civiles et des sentences arbitrales étrangères dans le droit de la republique socialiste de Roumanie', 16 *Revue roumaine des sciènces sociales – série de sciènces judiciaires* (1972) 285.
Filip, Ion, Capatina, Octavian, 'Les effets des sentences arbitrales étrangères en matière de rapports de commerce extérieur conformement en droit de la république socialiste de Roumanie', *Revue roumaine d'études internationales* (1967) 105. (Procedural aspects of arbitration in Rumania; the effect of international conventions.)

Saudi-Arabia

Moore, Michael T., Lott, Leslie J., 'Arbitration Under The Saudi Legal System' in a *Middle East Executive Reports* (February 1981), p. 11.

Spain

Brewer-Carias, Allan-Randolph, 'El control de las empreseas publicas por grupos de interesses de la communidad', 33 *Revue internationale des sciences administratives* (1967) 47.
——, *El regimen de las empressas publicas en el derecho comparado* (Caracas 1967).
Cremades, Bernardo Maria, 'Arbitraje Comercial International y Administaciones Publicas Espanolas' in Cremades, *Estudios sobre arbitraje* (Madrid 1977), p. 105. (State enterprises in Spain are not allowed to submit themselves to arbitration; permission of the Council of Ministers after hearing by the State Council (*Consejo de Estado*) is possible; submission to arbitration for a state enterprise engaged in international commerce is possible under Art. 2 of the European Convention of 21 April 1961.
Retortillo, Sebastiem Martin, 'Organisacion Administrativa de las empresas Publicas en Espagna', 32 *Revue internationale des sciences administratives* (1966) 1.

Sweden

Stockholm Chamber of Commerce (Publ.), *Arbitration in Sweden* (Stockholm 1977).

Union of Soviet Socialist Republics

Gause, Hermann, 'Die Entscheidung von Rechtsstreitigkeiten in Außenhandelsangelegenheiten der UdSSR', in Gause/Melsheimer (ed.), *Beiträge zum sowjetischen Außenhandelsrecht* (Berlin 1964), p. 7.
Gause, Hermann, Melsheimer, Klaus, *Beiträge zum sowjetischen Außenhandelsrecht*, Berichte des Osteuropa-Instituts an der Freien Universität Berlin – Reihe *Wirtschaft und Recht*. Heft 63 (Berlin 1964).

Genkin/Bogulawski, *Der Außenhandel und seine rechtliche Regelung in der UdSSR*, (East Berlin 1963).
Ginsburgs, George, 'Soviet International Trade Contracts and the Execution of Foreign Commercial Arbitral Awards' in D. Barry/W. Butler, G. Ginsburgs (ed.), *Contemporary Soviet Law. Essay in Honor of John N. Hazard* (The Hague 1974).
Goppold, Nikolaus, *Der Staatsbetrieb als juristische Person im sowjetischen Zivilrecht*, Diss. (Frankfurt/M. 1960).
Laptev, V. V., 'Rechtliche Stellung der sowjetischen Staatsbetriebe in der UdSSR', *Zeitschrift für das gesamte Handelsrecht und Wirtschaftsrecht* 134 (1970) 1. (General considerations on socialist enterprises; they belong to the people represented through the state; they fulfil the planning of the socialist republic.)
Larkin, E., 'The Effect of the Commission of International Trade Arbitration in the Soviet Union', 33 *George Washington Law Review* (1965) 728.
Lunc, L.A., 'Die Schiedsgerichtsbarkeit bei Streitigkeiten sowjetischer Wirtschaftsorganisationen mit kapitalistischen Unternehmen' (Originalsprache: russisch mit englischer Zusammenfassung), *Sovetskoe gosudarstvo i pravo* (1979) No. 2, pp. 50–54, 143.
Mina-Romer, Catherine, 'L'arbitrage de la Commission d'arbitrage pour le commerce extérieur de Moscou dans le commerce Est-Ouest', *Annuaire de L'U.R.S.S. et des pays socialistes européennes* (1978), p. 271.
Pfuhl, Eberhardt, 'Die Außenhandels- und Seearbitrage der UdSSR' Berichte des Osteuropa-Instituts an der Freien Universität Berlin, Heft 10, Reihe *Wirtschaft und Recht* (Berlin 1953).
Pomorski, S., 'State arbitration in the USSR: development, functions, organization', 9 *Rutger's Camden Law Journal* 61 (Fall 1977), 11.
Quigley, John, *The Soviet Foreign Trade Monopoly – Institutions and Laws*, (Ohio 1974). (History and function of Soviet Foreign Trade Monopoly; legal organization; *ultra vires* theory; low capitalization; very few physical assets; plant and equipment are 'basic assets', which are immune from execution under soviet law.)
Ramsaizew, D. F., *Die Außenhandelsarbitrage in der UdSSR* (Berlin 1961).
Roggemann, 'Die Gesetzgebung der sozialistischen Staaten', sub UdSSR 6.7.4.: Statut der Außenhandelsarbitrage bei der Kammer für Handel und Industrie der UdSSR, vom 16.4.1974.
Shpektorov, A. I., *Collected Arbitration Cases*. Awards of the Foreign Trade Arbitration commission, USSR Chamber of Commerce and Industry, Section of Law (Moscow 1972).
Waehler, Jan Peter, 'Die Außenhandels- und See- Schiedsgerichtsbarkeit in der UdSSR. Institutionen, Verfahren und Ermittlung des Anwendbaren Rechts', Osteuropa-Institut an der Freien Universität Berlin, *Rechtswissenschaftliche Abhandlungen*, Band 1 (Berlin, Baden-Baden 1974) (Foreign trade arbitration in the Soviet Union: evolution of the institution, legal form and structure of the foreign trade arbitration commission; competence and procedure of the commission; applicable law; enforcement).

United Kingdom

Coombes, David, *State Enterprises: Business or Politics* (London 1971).
Hauson, Albert H., *Public Enterprise and Economic Development* (London 1965).
John, William Tudor, 'Sovereign risk and immunity under English law and practice' in Rendell (ed.), *International Financial Law* (1980), p. 67.
Marshall, Enid A., 'The Arbitration Act 1979', *Journal of Bunnenhaw* (1979) 241 (247).
Martin-Pannetier, André, *Elements d'analyse comparative des établissements publics en droit français et en droit anglais* (Paris 1966).

United States of America

Crockett, Clyde H., 'Choice of law aspects of the Foreign Sovereign Immunity Act of 1976', 14 *Law and Policy in International Business* (1982) 1041.
Piney, 'Governmental Commercial Corporations', 11 *University of Cincinnati Law Review* (1937) 481.
Seidman, Harold, 'The Theory of the Autonomous Governmental Corporation, An Appraisal', 12 *Public Administration Review* (1952) 89.

Stevenson, John R., Browne, Jeffrey F., 'United States Law of sovereign immunity relating to international financial transactions' in Rendell (ed.), *International Financial Law* (1980), p. 85.

Yugoslavia

Conner, C., Vukmir, B., 'Legal Anatomy of a Yugoslav "Enterprise"', 32 *Business Lawyer* (1976) 99.

Goldštajn, A., *Međunaroda trgovačka arbitraža* (International Commercial Arbitration), Vol. I (Zagreb 1975); Vol. II (1976); Vol III (1977).

——, 'National Report – Yugoslavia' in *ICCA – Yearbook Commercial Arbitration* (P. Sanders, General Editor), Vol. I – 1976, p. 118.

——, *Državni akti i vanjskotrgovački ugovori* (The Effect of State Acts on Foreign Trade Contracts) (Zagreb 1966).

Grujić, Dusan, 'Die Vertretungsmacht in den jugoslawischen Unternehmen' in bfai (ed.), *Berichte und Dokumente zum ausländischen Wirtschafts- und Steuerrecht*, No. 135 a/b (December 1980), p. 50.

Jezdić, Michailo, 'La reconnaissance et l'exécution forcée des decisions judiciaires étrangères de caractère pecuniaire en vertu des conventions internationales multi-laterales', *Jugoslovenska Revija Za Medunarodno Pravo VII* (1960) 324.

Pretnar, Stojan, 'Das Unternehmen in Jugoslawien und seine Rechtsstellung', *Osteuropa-Recht* 7 (1961) 233. (The role and function of enterprise in the Yugoslav economy; special legal aspects: establishment and organization of the enterprise; separate legal and economic entity.)

Rithman, Zvone, 'Arbitration between Governments and Government Controlled Bodies and Foreign Business Firms', *Jugoslavenska Revija Za Medunarodno Pravo VII* (1960), 324.

Veltins, Michael, 'Durchgriffshaftung im amerikanischen Recht – Piercing the Corporate Veil', RIW (1983) 713.

A.4. REPORTS AND COMMENTS ON ARBITRATION OF SPECIFIC INTERNATIONAL INSTITUTIONS

ICSID

Amerasinghe, C. F., 'The International Center for Settlement of Investment Disputes and Development through the Multinational Corporation', *Vanderbilt Journal of Transnational Law* (1976) 793.

Broches, Aron, 'The Convention on the Settlement of Investment Disputes between States and Nationals of other States: Applicable Law and Default Procedure' in *Liber Amicorum for Martin Domke*, (The Hague 1967), p. 12.

——, *Investissements étrangers et arbitrage entre Etats et personnes privées: La Convention B.I.R.D. 18 mars 1965* (Paris 1969).

——, 'The Convention on the Settlement of Investment Disputes between States and Nationals of other States', Extract from the *Recueil des Cours*, Vol. II (1972).

Delaume, Georges E., 'Convention on the Settlement of Investment Disputes between States and Nationals of other States', *The International Lawyer* (1966).

——, 'Le CIRDI et l'immunité des Etats', *Revue de l'Arbitrage* (1983), No. 2, 143.

Firth, Thomas V., 'The Law Governing Contracts in Arbitration under the World Bank Convention' *New York University Journal of International Law and Politics* (1968) 253.

Kahn, 'The law applicable to foreign investments: the contribution of the World Bank Convention on the Settlement of Investment Disputes', 44 *Indiana Law Journal* (1968) 1.

Lauterpacht, 'The World Bank Convention on the Settlement of Investment Disputes' in *Homage to Paul Guggenheim* (Geneva 1968).

Masood, Arshad, 'Law Applicable in Arbitration of Investment Disputes under the World Bank Convention', 15 *Journal of the Indiana Law Institute* (1973) 311.

Sacerdotti, Giorgio, La Convenzione di Washington del 1965 per la soluzione delle controversie tra Stati e nazioni di altri Stati in materia di investimenti (The 1965 Washington Convention on Settlement of Investment Disputes between States and the Nationals of other States).

Schwarzenberger, G., 'The Arbitration Pattern and the Protection on Property Abroad' in *Liber Amicorum for Martin Domke* (The Hague 1967), p. 313.

Sutherland, 'The World Bank Convention on the Settlement of Investment Disputes', 28 *International and Comparative Law Quarterly*, (July 1979) 367.

IATA

Brancker, J. W. S., *IATA and what it does*. A factual description of the activities of the International Air Transport Association (Leyden 1977).

Brennan, Patrick, 'Upholding the tariff structure', 11 *IATA World Airline Cooperation Review*, No. 6 (June 1976) 8.

Chuang, Richard Y., *The International Air Transport Association*, (Leyden 1972).

Gidwitz, *The Politics of International Air Transport* (1980).

Haanappel, Peter P. C., *Ratemaking in International Air Transport* (Deventer 1978).

Larose, Aubry H., 'Reorganization and Restructuring of IATA', *Air Law* (1978) 252.

Reimer, 'The Role of Governments in Air Tariff Enforcement', *German Journal of Air and Space Law* (1982) 12.

Rudolf, Alfred, 'Neuere Entwicklungen betreffend die IATA', *German Journal of Air and Space Law*, (1979) 175.

Schoner, 'IATA, 34. Jahreshauptversammlung, Genf 13–15. November 1978', *German Journal of Air and Space Law* (1979) 34.

Schwenck, Walter, *Handbuch des Luftverkehrsrechts* (Köln . . . 1981).

B. CASES

B.1. ARBITRATION CASES

B.1.1. International Chamber of Commerce

International Chamber of Commerce, Arbitral Tribunal

Award 1455/1967, *Yearbook Commercial Arbitration*, vol. III (1978), p. 215. Arbitrator applies the private international law of the forum; interventions of public authorities and their impact on international contracts.

Award 1529/1968, *Journal de droit international (Clunet)* (1974), p. 915.

Award 1598/1971, *Yearbook Commercial Arbitration*, vol. III (1978), p. 216. Applicable law.

Award 2091 May 14, 1972, *Revue de l'Arbitrage* (1975), p. 253, note Fouchard, p. 258. 'Clause compromissoire' between a French company and an international organization; immunity of jurisdiction autonomy of the arbitral clause.

Award 1803/1972: *Société des Grands Travaux de Marseille (France)* v. *East Pakistan Industrial Development Corporation*, *Yearbook Commercial Arbitration*, vol. V (1980), p. 177. Jurisdiction of arbitrator; law governing arbitration; dissolution of party governing arbitration; confiscatory measures by state; public policy.

Award 2139/1974, *Yearbook Commercial Arbitration*, vol. III (1978), p. 220. *Force majeure* claimed by a foreign enterprise towards a state enterprise; nationalization.

Award 2216/1974, unpublished, available at the Cologne University Chair of International Business Law.

Sent. arb. 2321/1974, *Journal de droit international (Clunet)* (1975), p. 938, note, p. 940. State and state enterprise engaged in international transactions; dismissal of immunity defence before the arbitral tribunal sitting in Sweden.

Award 2478/1974, *Yearbook Commercial Arbitration*, vol. III (1978), p. 222, *Journal de droit international (Clunet)* (1975), p. 925. Re-adaptation clause in a contract of a Rumanian seller and a French buyer; cancellation of the export licence by Rumanian authorities constitutes a case of *force majeure*.

Sent. arb. 1434/1975, *Journal de droit international (Clunet)* (1976), p. 978. Contracts between a state enterprise of a LDC and a 'group des sociétés'; applicable law.

Sent. arb. 2521/1975, *Journal de droit international (Clunet)* (1976), p. 997. 'Etablissement public'. Aptitude à compromettre.

Saudi-Arabia v. *Arabian American Oil Co. (Aramco)*, Aug. 23, 1958, 27 I.L.R. 117–233.

Libyan American Oil Company (Liamco) v. *The Government of the Libyan Arab Republic*, April 12, 1977, 20 *Intern. Legal Materials* (1981) 1.

Award 2903/1978: *Afiometal (Syria)* v. *Röchling (FR Germany)*, not published.

Award rendered in cases no. 2977–2978–3033 on April 5, 1978: *AB Götaverken* v. *Libyan General Maritime Transport Organization succeeded by General Maritime Transport Company*, published in J. G. Wetter, *The International Arbitral Process*, vol. II, 1979, p. 209, *Yearbook Commercial Arbitration*, vol. VI, p. 133.

Award 3011/1978, *Afiometal (Syria)* v. *Lessoimpex (Bulgaria)*, not published.

Sentence rendue dans l'affaire 3093/3100 en 1979, *Journal de droit international* (*Clunet*) (1981), p. 951, avec *observations*. Contract between two public enterprises of two African countries; refusal of the central bank to allow export currency; no case of *force majeure* because public enterprise is the same 'entité juridique' as the state (and also the central bank).

Award 3259/1980: *Compass International (Lebanon)* v. *General Company for the Manufacture of Synthetic Detergents (Syria)*, not published.

Award 3530/1980: *A.B.R. (Belgium)* v. *GOFS (Syria)*, not published.

B.1.2. Foreign Trade Arbitration Courts in Socialist Countries

Bulgaria

COURT OF ARBITRATION AT THE BULGARIAN CHAMBER OF COMMERCE AND INDUSTRY

Award April 25, 1972, 91/1970, *Yearbook Commercial Arbitration* vol. IV (1979), p. 189 (no. 2). Competence of Court of Arbitration despite the lack of written arbitration agreement.

Award May 12, 1972, 80/1970, *Yearbook Commercial Arbitration*, vol. IV (1979), p. 191 (no. 5). Arbitrator's power to decide on his own competence.

Cour arbitrale, 24.6.1972, 68/1971, *Journal de droit international* (*Clunet*) (1978), p. 653, note. 'Capacité d'ester en justice', 'capacité d'exercise' of a foreign enterprise (Hungarian); application of *lex patriae*.

Award Oct. 25, 1972, 40/1972, *Yearbook Commercial Arbitration*, vol. IV (1979), p. 190 (no. 4). Time limit for initiating arbitration.

Award June 23, 1973, 88/1972, *Yearbook Commercial Arbitration*, vol. IV (1979), p. 189 (no. 3). Autonomy of arbitration clause.

Award Nov. 3, 1973, 152/1972, *Yearbook Commercial Arbitration*, vol. IV (1979), p. 191 (no. 6). Bankruptcy of party during arbitration does not deprive arbitration court from its competence.

Award Nov. 12, 1974, 128/1973, *Yearbook Commercial Arbitration*, vol. IV (1979), p. 188, *Journal de droit international* (*Clunet*) (1978), p. 633; note, p. 634. Nationality of a company; majority participation of Bulgarian state enterprises in the assets of a company does not make this company a (Bulgarian) legal person.

Kojouharoff, Al., 'Chronique de jurisprudence de la Cour arbitrale près la Chambre de commerce bulgare', *Journal de droit international* (*Clunet*) (1967), p. 152.

Stalev, J., 'Chronique de jurisprudence de la Cour arbitrale près la Chambre de commerce et d'industrie de Bulgarie (I)', *Journal de droit international* (*Clunet*) (1978), p. 633.

Czechoslovakia

ARBITRATION COURT AT THE CHAMBER OF COMMERCE OF CZECHOSLOVAKIA

Sentence No. 117/70, June 22, 1971, *Revue de l'Arbitrage* (1974), p. 41.

Sentence no. 51/71, Aug. 5, 1971, *Revue de l'Arbitrage* (1974), p. 39.

Sentence no. 121/69, Aug. 28, 1971, *Revue de l'Arbitrage* (1974), p. 35.

Sentence no. 129/69, Dec. 21, 1971, *Revue de l'Arbitrage* (1974), p. 42.

Sentence no. 106/68, Feb. 16, 1972, *Revue de l'Arbitrage* (1974), p. 29.

Sentence no. 79/71, March 20, 1972, *Revue de l'Arbitrage* (1974), p. 33.

Award Oct. 5, 1973, RSP 130/170. *Yearbook Commercial Arbitration* (1976), p. 125. Obligation of the Czechoslovakien party to provide the official authorization; no *force majeure* defence.

Award Jan. 5, 1977, *Yearbook Commercial Arbitration*, vol. IV (1979), p. 194. Application of Act No. 101/Dec. 4, 1963, concerning Legal Relations in International Trade; objective liability.

Award Oct. 10, 1979, RSP 113/79, *Yearbook Commercial Arbitration*, vol. VI (1981), p. 126. Competence of arbitration court; applicable law on arbitration.

German Democratic Republic

ARBITRAL COURT ATTACHED TO THE CHAMBER OF FOREIGN TRADE OF THE G.D.R.

Award: SG 257/71, 31.10.1972, in *Kammer für Außenhandel der DDR* (ed.), p. 57.

Award: SG 284/74, 20.10.1975, in *Kammer für Außenhandel der DDR* (ed.), Aus der Spruchpraxis des Schiedsgerichts bei der Kammer für Außenhandel der DDR (1969–1976), (East Berlin 1977), p. 51.

Award SG 103/74, 28.1.1976: *VEB K. RDA* c. *Entreprise WRFA, Journal de droit international* (*Clunet*) (1980), p. 696.

Award SG 246/75, 16.7.1976, *Yearbook Commercial Arbitration* vol. II (1977), p. 144.

Hungary

Décision no. 34, November 29, 1958, *Journal de droit international* (*Clunet*) (1968), p. 426.

Farago, pp. 15, 16, 18, *Journal de droit international* (*Clunet*) (1973), p. 488. Hungarian enterprise must prove *force majeure*; ministerial decision does not constitute a *force majeure* – case; embargo.

Poland

COURT OF ARBITRATION AT THE POLISH CHAMBER OF FOREIGN TRADE IN WARSAW

Award Feb. 11, 1958, case no. 17/57, *Yearbook Commercial Arbitration*, vol. VI (1981), p. 147, IX *Polish Yearbook of International Law*, (1977–78) (Warsaw 1980), p. 267. Even in a socialist system there is no liability of an enterprise for acts of state because it has a distinct legal personality from the latter.

Award June 16, 1969, case no. 605/68, IX *Polish Yearbook of International Law* (1977–78), p. 289. The recourse claim between the enterprises from CMEA countries for costs borne in a certain currency must be satisfied in the same currency and not in transferable roubles.

Award October 13, 1969, case no. 595/68, IX *Polish Yearbook of International Law*, (1977–1978), p. 289. Damages caused by the devaluation of the contract's currency may not be adjudged except under a preventive currency clause.

Award November 3, 1974, Case no. 789/71, *Yearbook Commercial Arbitration*, Vol. I, 1976, p. 139. Damages for non-performance of the contract; 'moral losses' under Bulgarian law; choice of arbitration forum by claimant; Belgian company–Bulgarian foreign trade enterprise.

Award July 7, 1976, case no. 134/74, *Yearbook Commercial Arbitration*, vol. III (1978), p. 228. Liability of surveyor.

POLISH CHAMBER OF FOREIGN TRADE

Zorzecznictwa Kolegium Arbitrów przy Polskiej Izbie Handlu Zagranicznego (Warschau 1980); A collection of selected cases, published by Cz. Przymusiński.

Union of Soviet Socialist Republics

FOREIGN TRADE ARBITRATION COMMISSION

Lena Goldfields Co. Ltd. v. *Union of Socialist Soviet Republics*, award, *International Law Reports* 1929/30, pp. 3 and 426; *British Yearbook of International Law* 1957, p. 10.

Award 20.5.1940: *Joint Stock Company Fanto Petroleum Maatchapij (Amsterdam)* v. *V/O Soiuzneftexport* in USSR Chamber of Commerce and Industry, Law Section (ed.), *Collected Arbitration Cases*, part I, 'Awards of the FTAC 1934–1951' (Moscow 1972), p. 72. Representation of soviet export trade enterprises.

Award 6.3.1941: *V/O Raznoimport* v. *the Bulgarian Joint-Stock Company Musalla and Trading House Serdika* in USSR Chamber of Commerce and Industry, Law Section (ed.), *Collected Arbitration Cases*, part I, 'Awards of the FTAC 1934–1951' (Moscow 1972), p. 79.

Award 27.2.1950: *V/O Exportless* v. *Joint-Stock Company Intercontinental de Bois Rouphine Pierrard (Gilly, Belgium)*, in: USSR Chamber of Commerce and Industry, Law Section (ed.), *Collected Arbitration Cases*, part I, 'Awards of the FTAC 1934–1951' (Moscow 1972), p. 102. Jurisdiction of the FTAC (voluntary).

Award 27.10.1950: *V/O Stankoimport* v. *The Joint-Stock Company Swisstool (Zurich, Switzerland)*, in USSR Chamber of commerce and Industry, Law Section (ed.), *Collected Arbitration Cases*, part I, 'Awards of the FTAC 1934–1951' (Moscow 1972), p. 115. Nature of the USSR

Chamber of Commerce and Industry; social organization; not governmental body; its members are arbiters not state officials.

Award (Moscow) 3.7.1958: *Jordan Investment Ltd. (Israel)* v. *All-Union Foreign Trade Corporation (USSR)*, 53 *American Journal of International Law* (1959) 800.

Award 6.10.1977, *Yearbook Commercial Arbitration* vol. V (1980), p. 209. Disputes between a soviet foreign trade enterprise and a Sri Lanka firm; applicable law; letter of credit.

B.1.3. Ad Hoc Arbitration

Administration of Posts and Telegraphs of the Republic of Czechoslovakia v. *Radio Corporation of U.S.A.*, award 1.4.1932 (Jul. Möller), 30 *American Journal of International Law* (1936) 523. Applicable law; the state could be able to show that public interests of vital importance would suffer if the agreement should be upheld under the rules of ordinary civil law.

Yugoslavia v. *Société Européenne d'Etudes ed d'Enterprises*, award 2.7.1956 (Ripert et Panchaud), 24 *International Law Review* (1957), p. 761, *Journal de droit international (Clunet)* (1959), 1074/80. Arbitration clause in contract between commercial firm and state; binding force on arbitrators of exchange of letters between that state and government of the firm.

Sapphire International Petroleum Ltd. v. *National Iranian Oil Company*, arbitral award 15.3.1963 (unpublished available at the Cologne University Chair of International Business Law).

B.1.4. ICSID Arbitration

Case ARB/72/1: *Holiday Inns/Occidental Petroleum* v. *Government of Morocco*, *ICSID Annual Report*, 1980/81, p. 30.

Case ARB/74/1: *Adriano Gardella SpA* v. *Government of Ivory Coast*, *ICSID Annual Report*, 1980/81, p. 33.

Case ARB/74/2: *Alcoa Minerals of Jamaica, Inc.* v. *Government of Jamaica*, *ICSID Annual Report*, 1980/81, p. 34.

Case ARB/74/3: *Kaiser Bauxite Company* v. *Government of Jamaica*, ICSID Annual Report, 1980/81, p. 36.

Case ARB/74/4: *Reynolds Jamaica Mines Ltd. and Reynolds Metals Company* v. *Government of Jamaica*, *ICSID Annual Report*, 1980/81, p. 37.

Case ARB/76/1: *Government of Gabon* v. *Société Serete S.A.*, *ICSID Annual Report*, 1980/81, p. 39.

Case ARB/77/1: *AGIP SpA* v. *Government of the People's Republic of the Congo*, *ICSID Annual Report*, 1980/81, p. 39.

Case ARB/77/2: *Société Ltd. Benvenuti & Bonfant srl.* v. *Government of the People's Republic of the Congo*, *ICSID Annual Report*, 1980/81, p. 40.

Case ARB/78/1: *Guadalupe Gas Products Corporation* v. *Federal Military Government of Nigeria*, *ICSID Annual Report*, 1980/81, p. 42.

Case ARB/81/1: *AMCO Asia Corporation, Pan American Development Ltd. and P.T. AMCO Indonesia* v. *Government of Indonesia*.

Case ARB/81/2: *Klöckner Industrie-Anlage GmbH, Klöckner Belge, S.A. and Klöckner Handels-maatschappij B.V.* v. *United Republic of Cameroon.*

B.1.5. Iran–USA Claims Tribunal

Decisions and awards are available at the Iran–USA Claims Tribunal, 13 Parkweg, 2582 JH The Hague, Netherlands, tel (070) 52.00.64; but also published in: *Iranian Assets Litigation Reporter* (Edgemont/Pennsylvania).

This Arbitral Tribunal was established on the basis of the Declaration of the Government of the Democratic and Popular Republic of Algeria, Concerning the Settlement of Claims by the Government of the United States of America and the Government of the Islamic Republic of Iran, January 19, 1981. According to Article II of this declaration the Tribunal deals with claims of nationals of the USA against Iran and of nationals of Iran against the USA, and claims of the USA and Iran against each other arising out of contractual arrangements between them for the purchase and sale of goods and services.

B.2. DECISIONS OF NATIONAL COURTS

Australia

The Australian Mutual Provident Society v. *Overseas Telecommunications (Australia)* [1972] 2 NSWLR 806.

Bailey v. *Commissioner of Taxation* (1977) 51 ALJR 429.

Blomen (P. J.) Pty. Ltd. v. *The Council of the City of Gold Coast* [1973] AC 115.

Bonython v. *Commonwealth of Australia* [1951] AC 201.

Brisbane City Council v. *Albert House Limited (in voluntary liquidation)*, (1968) 42 ALJR 158.

Broten v. *Randwick Municipal Council* [1964–1965] NSWR 1445.

Canterbury Pipelines (Aust.) Pty. Ltd. v. *Gold Coast (City) Council* (1968) 118 CLR 58.

Civil and Civic Pty. Ltd. v. *Minister for Works for Government of Western Australia* (1967) 116 CLR 273.

The Commonwealth Government v. *Adelaide Steamship Industries* (1974) 24 FLR 97.

Construction Services Pty. Ltd. v. *Lithgow City Council* [1967] SR(NSW), 579.

Conway v. *Rimmer* [1968] AC 940.

Driver v. *War Service Homes Commissioner* 24 VLR(No. 1) 514.

Gas & Fuel Corporation of Victoria v. *Wood Hall Ltd. & Liquid Pipeline Constructors Ltd.* [1978] VR 385.

Heiman v. *Commonwealth of Australia* (1938) 38 SR(NSW) 691.

Henry v. *Uralla Municipal Council* (1934) 35 SR(NSW) 15.

Kidman v. *Commonwealth* (1923) 23 SR(NSW) 329.

Kirby v. *Sutherland Shire Council* [1961] NSWR 718.

Leighton Constructors v. *Western Australian Government Railways Commissioner* (1966) 115 CLR 575.

Muusers and another v. *State Government Insurance Office (Queensland)*, [1980] 2 NSWLR 75.

Ryde Municipal Council ex parte, re v. *Norton Tin Printers* (1959) 5 LGRA 83.

Serphina Bell Pty. Ltd. v. *Willoughby Municipal Council* [1967] NSWR 413.

Slapjones v. *City of Knox (no. 1)* [1978] VR 325.

South Australian Railways Commissioner v. *Egan*, (1972) 130 CLR 506.

Sydney City Council v. *West* (1965) 114 CLR, 481).

Federal Republic of Germany

BGH

9.12.1958 (Akt. 7 VIII ZR 80/56) (*Volkswagen Savers Case*).

6.3.1969, *Yearbook Commercial Arbitration*, vol. II (1977), p. 235; *Wertpapier Mitteilungen* (1969) 671; *Der Betrieb* (1969), 922; *Monatsschrift für Deutsches Recht* (1969) 567; *Konkurs-Treuhand-Schiedsgerichtswesen* 31 (1970) 30; Die deutsche Rechtssprechung auf dem Gebiete des IPR 1968–1969, no. 256.

Urt. 23.9.1969, VI ZR 19/68, BGHZ 52, 325, *Die Offentliche Verwaltung* (1970) 61.

BayVGH

Urt. 4.10.1976, Nr. 42 XIV 73, *Bayerisches Verwaltungsblatt* (1977) 469. Definition of a 'wirtschaftliches Unternehmen' of a commune.

Kammergericht

26.11.1954, IPR-Rechtsprechung 1954/55 Nr. 28.

OLG Bremen

Beschl. 22.3.1977, 2 W 102/75; *Die Öffentliche Verwaltung* (1977) 899, note Püttner 901.

OLG Frankfurt/M.

U. 19.5.1959, 4 U 217/58, *Außenwirtschaftsdienst* (1960), p. 217. Arbitrators members of a state enterprise in Yugoslavia. No violation of 'ordre public'.

Beschl. v. 21.10.80, 5 W 24/80 IPrax 1981, p. 71.

11.5.1981, 20 W 422/80, *Recht der Internationalen Wirtschaft/Außenwirtschaftsdienst* (1981), p. 484. The National Iranian Oil Company is not entitled to immunity; it is a separate juridical person acting on commercial law principles; it is not to be identified with the Iranian State.

OLG Hamburg

14.10.1964, *Yearbook Commercial Arbitration*, vol. II (1977), p. 235, Die deutsche Rechtssprechung auf dem Gebiete des IPR 1964–1965, no. 277.

8.5.1969, IPR-Rechtsprechung 1971, Nr. 158a; *Wertpapiermitteilungen* 1969, p. 709.

OLG Karlsruhe

Urt. 14.11.1979, 6 U 161/78, *Recht der Internationalen Wirtschaft/Außenwirtschaftsdienst des Betriebsberaters*. Submission of a foreign state to German jurisdiction.

OLG Koblenz

10.10.1972 IPR-Rechtsprechung 1974, Nr. 1a; *Entscheidungen der Oberlandesgerichte in Zivilsachen* (OLGZ) (1975), p. 379.

France

Conseil Constitutionel

9.4.1964, *Actualité Juridique Droit Administratif* (1964) II, 302.

Conseil d'Etat

17.3.1893, *Chemins de Fer du Nord*, JCP – *Semaine juridique* (1899) III, 123.

Conseil d'Etat (Section du Contentieux)

13.12.1957, *Société Nationale de Vente de Surplus*, *Revue de l'Arbitrage* (1958), p. 20. Public enterprises are not allowed to submit to arbitration.

Cour de Cassation

3.11.1952, *Epoux Martin* c. *Bounque d'Espagne*, *Revue critique de droit international Privé* 53, 425.

14.4.1964, *Office National Interprofessionnel des Céréales* c. *Capitaine du SS. San Carlo*, *Revue de l'Arbitrage* (1964), p. 82, *Journal de droit international* (*Clunet*) (1965), p. 646.

2.5.1966, *Trésor Public* c. *Galakis*, *Dalloz* 1966, p. 575, note Robert; *Revue critique de droit international privé* (1967), p. 553, note Goldmann; *Journal de droit international* (*Clunet*) (1966), p. 648, note Level; JCP – *Semaine juridique* (1966) II 14798, note Ligneau; *Revue de l'Arbitrage* (1966), p. 99. Public enterprises may submit to arbitration in the presence of an international contract.

14.2.1978, *Crédit populaire d'Algérie* c. *SAPVIN*, *Revue critique de droit international privé*, vol. 69 (1980), p. 707, note Mayer.

2.5.1978, *Sociétè algérienne de commerce Alco et autres* c. *Sempac et autres*, *Journal de droit international* (*Clunet*) (1978), p. 904, note Ph. Kahn. Grant of immunity to an Algerian national corporation acting in representation of the Algerian state.

Cass. civ. (1re Ch.) 19.3.1979, *Bulletin civil*, IV, no. 104, p. 80; *Revue critique de droit international privé* (1980), p. 836 sommaire. No immunity from jurisdiction or execution for a foreign state enterprise engaged in international commerce.

Cour d'Appel de Paris

29.1.1975, *Société Européenne d'Etudes et d'Entreprises* c. *Republique socialiste fédérale de Yougoslavie, Ministre Francais des affaires étrangères, Banque mondiale*, (1975), *Revue de l'Arbitrage* p. 328, note Delvolvé.

4.5.1976, *Engel* c. *Coopérative agricole de la Mense*, *Revue de l'Arbitrage*, p. 261. 'Sociétés coopératives agricoles' can submit to arbitration (art. 1 V) 'ordonance' 26.9.1967 modified through law of 27.6.1972.

21.2.1980, *General National Maritime Transport Company* c. *Société GÖTAVERKEN ARENDAL A.B.*, *Yearbook Commercial Arbitration*, vol. VI (1981), p. 221; *Journal de droit international* (*Clunet*) (1980), p. 660, note Fouchard, *Revue critique de droit international* (1980), p. 763; *Revue de l'Arbitrage* (1980), p. 524, note Jeantel.

Tribunal de grande instance de Paris

14.5.1970, *Gazette de Palais* (1971), 1, 17.

6.7.1970, *Rep. soc. fed. de Yougoslavie* c. *Société européenne d'études et d'entreprises*, *Journal de droit international* (*Clunet*) (1971), p. 131, note Ph. Kahn p. 134. Court refuses *exequatur* of a foreign arbitral award rendered against a socialist state enterprise.

29.11.1972, *Corporacion del Cobre* c. *Société Braden Copper Corporation et Société Le Groupement d'importation des Métaux*, *Journal de droit international* (*Clunet*) (1973), p. 227, note Ph. Kahn. Submission of a state enterprise to arbitration is valuable; no state immunity for it acting in international commerce.

Iran

First Instance Court of Tehran

Decision December 1, 1963, *National Iranian Oil Company* v. *Sapphire International Petroleums Ltd.*, *9 International Legal Materials* (1970) 1118.

Italy

Cour de Cassation

4 Avril 1978, No. 1540 dans *Foro Italiano* (1979) 1, 768.

18 Décembre 1973, No. 3433 dans *Giustizia Civile* (1974) 1, 1110.

Collège Arbitral de Turin

26 Octobre 1974 dans *Arbitrage et Marchés* (1975) 279.

Trib. G. I. Palermo

19 Février 1972 dans *Giurisprudenza Italiana* (1973) 1, C, 547.

Luxembourg

Tribunal d'arrondissement

6.12.1933, TômeXIII, page 218.

Netherlands

Supreme Court of the Netherlands

Oct. 26, 1973, *Revue de l'Arbitrage* (1974), p. 318, note Batiffol, p. 326. State immunity of jurisdiction and of execution; the New York Convention 1958 is applicable to states non-members of the Convention; interpretation of Art. V, §1, of the Convention.

Hague Court of Appeal

Nov. 28, 1968, NV *Cabolent* v. *National Iranian Oil Company*, 9 *International Legal Materials* (1970) 152 (English translation); *Nederlandse Jurisprudentie* (1969) No. 484, p. 1329.

Sept. 8, 1972, *Revue de l'Arbitrage* (1974), p. 313. Immunity of jurisdiction and of execution; interpretation of the New York Convention 1958.

Oct. 25, 1974, *Revue de l'Arbitrage* (1974), p. 322.

President of Rechtbank, Amsterdam

Dec. 14, 1977, *Yearbook Commercial Arbitration*, vol. IV (1979), p. 307. Power of the state to represent a state enterprise (rejected); application of New York Convention.

District Court of The Hague

April 15, 1965, *NV Cabolent* v. *National Iranian Oil Company*, 5 *International Legal Materials* (1966), p. 477.

Sweden

Supreme Court of Sweden

Aug. 13, 1979, *AB Götaverken (Swedish)* v. *General National Maritime Transport Company (GMTC), Libya, legal successor of Libyan General Maritime Transport Organization (GMTO)*, *Yearbook Commercial Arbitration*, vol. VI (1981), p. 237 (239).

Svea Court of Appeal (5th Dep.) Stockholm

Dec. 13, 1978, *AB Götaverken (Swedish)* v. *General National Maritime Transport Company*

(GMTC), Libya, legal successor of Libyan General Maritime Transport Organization (GMTO), Yearbook Commercial Arbitration, vol. VI (1981), p. 237.

Switzerland

Schweizerisches Bundesgericht

12.2.1958 in Sachen *Ligna gegen Baumgartner*, BGE 84 I 39, *Außenwirtschaftsdienst* (1958), pp. 185–187. Arbitration in Czechoslovakia; arbitrators members of a state chamber of commerce; award against a Swiss enterprise; no violation of *ordre public*.

3.5.1967, BGE 93 (1967), p. 265, *Yearbook Commercial Arbitration*, 1976, p. 200. Enforcement of an award rendered by the Arbitration Court attached to the Chamber of Commerce in Berlin – East.

17.3.1975, *Jugomineral* c. *Grillo Werbe AG, Journal de droit international* (*Clunet*) (1976), p. 729.

21.5.1975, *Verband der Schlittschuh und Rollschuhsporte Jugoslawiens* c. *Gschwend, Journal de droit international* (*Clunet*) (1976), p. 732.

5.5.1976, *Société des grands travaux de Marseille contre Republique populaire du Bangladesh, Bangladesh industrial development corporation, Annuaire du Tribunal Fédéral* 102 Ia, p. 574; *Yearbook Commercial Arbitration*, vol. V (1980), p. 217. Applicable law; there is no violation of *ordre public* if a foreign state does not recognize arbitration agreements signed by a confiscated enterprise.

19.6.1980, *Libyan American Co.* v. *Libyan Arabia Republic*, 20 *International Legal Materials* (1981), p. 151. The court refuses to recognize and enforce the award rendered against Libya, because there is no connection between the arbitration and Switzerland.

OG Zürich (III Zivilkammer)

19.2.1958, *Schweizerische Juristen Zeitung* (1958), p. 199; *Außenwirtschaftsdienst* (1958), p. 188.

United Kingdom

House of Lords

Czarnikow Ltd. v. *Centrala Handlu Zagranicznego 'Rolimpex'* [1978] 2 *All England Reports* 1043. Government intervention beyond seller's control; seller a state trading organization; identity of government seller state organization separate legal entity.

Court of Appeal

Krajina v. *The Tass Agency* [1949] 2 *All England Reports* 274.

William Cory and Son, Ltd. v. *City of London Corporation* [1951] 2 *All England Reports* 85. 'Where a statute confers power on any body, whether one which is seeking to make a profit for shareholders or one acting solely for the public good, . . . purporting to bring such a body and their successors not to use the powers is void'.

Baccus SRL v. *Servicio Nacional Del Trigo*, [1956] 3 *Weekly Law Reports* 948.

Mellenger v. *New Brunswick Development Corporation* [1971] 1 *Weekly Law Reports* 604. 'A corporation, though a separate legal entity, is entitled to sovereign immunity if there is a close connection with the government, it is carrying out the latter's policy and did not carry on any commercial transaction' (Lord Denning, MR).

Trendtex Trading Corp. Ltd. v. *Central Bank of Nigeria* [1977] 1 *All England Reports* 881.

C. Czarnikow Ltd. v. *Centrala Handlu Zagranicznego 'Rolimpex'* [1978] 1 *All England Reports* 81. Seller a state trading organization; identity of government and seller; state organization separate legal entity and not entitled to claim sovereign immunity but under supervision and accountable to department of Polish Government.

1° Congreso del Partido [1980] 1 *Lloyd's List Law Reports* 23.

Queen's Bench Division

Trendtex Trading Corporation v. *Central Bank of Nigeria*, (1975 T. No. 3663) *Donaldson Journal*, [1976] 1 *Weekly Law Reports* 868. The Central Bank of Nigeria is an *alter ego* and a department of the State of Nigeria; its acting in trade does not mean a waiver of state immunity for the State of Nigeria; state immunity.

1° Congreso del Partido [1978] 1 *All England Reports* 1161.

Privy Council

Metropolitan Meat Industry Board v. *Sheedy*, [1927] *Law Reports AC* 899. Incorporated board with wide powers given to be exercised at its own discretion and without consulting the direct representatives of the Crown; there is no identity with the Crown.

United States of America

Supreme Court of the United States

23.3.1964, *Banco Nacional de Cuba* v. *Sabbatino*, 376 US 398, 84 S.Ct. 923. Sovereign immunity claimed by instrumentality of a foreign state; expropriation.

Alfred Dunhill of London, Inc. v. *Republic of Cuba*, decided May 24, 1976, 15 *International Legal Materials* (1976), p. 735; 425 US 682 (1976); 70 *American Journal of International Law* 828 (1977).

Ulen & Co. v. *National Economic Bank*, Supreme Court 1940, 24 N.Y.S. 2d 106.

Milwaukee Refrigerator Transit Co. v. *United States of America*, 142 F. 247, 255 (C.C.Wis. 1905).

North Arlington Medical Building Inc. v. *Sanchez Construction Co.*, 86 Nev. 515, 520; 471 P. 2d 240, 243 (1970).

Banco National de Cuba v. *First National City Bank of New York*, 270 F.Supp. 1004 (1967).

Banca P.C.E. de Cuba v. *First National City Bank*, 505 F.Supp. 412 (1980).

United States District Court (North District of Illinois)

Rovin Sales Corp. v. *Socialist Republic of Rumania*, 403 F.Supp. 1298.

United States District Court (District of Columbia)

Edlow International Company v. *Nuklearna Elektrarnna Krsko*, 441 F.Supp. 827.

Maritime International Nominees Establishment v. *The Republic of Guinea*, Memorandum Jan. 12, 1981, 20 *International Legal Materials* (1981), p. 669. Agreeing to arbitration before arbitrators selected by the president of ICSID Guinea waived its immunity; since the other partner to the contract was an enterprise from a state non-member of ICSID, arbitration was brought to the American Arbitration Association.

Iptrade International S. A. (France) v. *Federal Republic of Nigeria*, Sept. 25, 1978, 17 *International Legal Materials* (1970), pp. 1395–1401; *Yearbook of Commercial Arbitration*, vol. IV (1979), p. 337. Application of New York Convention; no sovereign immunity in favour of foreign state.

Icenogle v. *Olympic Airways*, March 19, 1979, 18 *International Legal Materials* (1979), p. 963.

United States District Court (District of New Jersey)

Behring International v. *Imperial Iranian Air Force*, July 24, 1979, 18 *International Legal Materials* (1979), p. 1370.

United States District Court (Southern District of New York)

Yessih-Volpih v. *Novosti Press Agency*, 433 F.Supp. 849.

Jugometal (Yugoslavia) v. *Samincorp., Inc (USA)*, Apr. 21, 1978, case no. 77 Civ. 5569 – CLB, *Yearbook Commercial Arbitration*, vol. IV (1979), p. 334. Enforcement of arbitration awards in favour of a Yugoslav enterprise in U.S.A.

Reading and Bates v. *National Iranian Oil Company*, 18 *International Legal Materials* (1979), p. 1398.

Amoco Overseas Oil Co. v. *Compagnie Nationale Algérienne de Navigation*, Sept., 27, 1978, 18 *International Legal Materials* (1979), p. 109.

East Europe Domestic International Sales Corporation v. *Terra*, March 13, 1979, 18 *International Legal Materials* (1979), p. 977.

United States Court of Appeal (2nd Circuit)

Texas Trading & Milling Co. v. *Federal Republic of Nigeria and Central Bank of Nigeria*, April 16, 1981, 20 *International Legal Materials* (1981), p. 619.

United States Court of Appeal (5th Circuit)

Imperial Ethiopian Government v. *Basuch Foster Corporation*, July 19, 1976, 535 F. 2d 334; in

Giorgio Gaja (ed.) *International Commercial Arbitration* v. *New York Convention*, V. 37 i, (New York 1979).

United States Court of Appeal
Sperry International Trade v. *Israel*, September 3, 1982, 19 *International Legal Materials*, (1982), p. 1066.

B.3. CASES DEALING WITH CERTAIN ASPECTS OF THE TOPIC

B.3.1. Determination of the applicable law

Sapphire International Petroleum Ltd. v. *National Iranian Oil Company*, arbitral award 15.3.1963, unpublished available at the Cologne University Chair of International Business Law. No distinction between the state and a state enterprise in respect of the applicable substantive law; since the 'state' (here NIOC) is involved the general principles of international law are applicable.

International Chamber of Commerce, Arbitral Tribunal
Award case no. 2216/1974, unpublished available at the Cologne University Chair of International Business Law.
Award rendered in cases nos. 2977, 2978, 3033 on April 5, 1978, *AB Götaverken* v. *Libyan General Maritime Transport Organization succeeded by General Maritime Transport Company*, published in J. G. Wetter, *The International Arbitral Process*, vol. 2 (1979), p. 209; *Yearbook Commercial Arbitration*, vol. VI (1981), p. 133.
Sent. arb. 1434/1975, *Journal de droit international* (*Clunet*) (1976), p. 978.
Award 1598/1971, *Yearbook Commercial Arbitration* vol. III (1978), p. 216. Danish corporation against Bulgarian and Ethiopian enterprises.
Award no. 1455/1967, *Yearbook Commercial Arbitration*, vol. III (1978), p. 215.

Court of Arbitration at the Bulgarian Chamber of Commerce and Industry
Cour arbitrale, 24.6.1972, 68/1971, *Journal de droit international* (*Clunet*) (1978), p. 653, note.

Arbitration court at the Chamber of Commerce of Czechoslovakia
Sentence 129/69, Dec. 21, 1971, *Revue de l'Arbitrage* (1974), p. 42.
Sentence 117/70, June 22, 1971, *Revue de l'Arbitrage* (1974), p. 41.
Award Oct. 10, 1979, case no. RSP.113/79, *Yearbook Commercial Arbitration*, vol. VI (1981), p. 126.

Kammergericht, Fed. Rep. of Germany
26.11.1954 IPR-Rechtsprechung 1954/55, Nr. 28.

Arbitral Court attached to the Chamber of Foreign Trade of the GDR
Award SG 246/75, 16.7.1976, *Yearbook Commercial Arbitration*, vol. II (1977), p. 144.
Award, SG 103/74, 28.1.76 *VEB K. RDA* v. *Enterprise WRFA*, *Journal de droit international* (*Clunet*) (1980), p. 696.

Cassation administratif (Libya)
2.5.1971, *Libyan Arab Republic, Supreme Court Journal*, 8 I (1971–1972), p. 5.
20.6.1971, *Supreme Court Journal*, 8 I, p. 11.

Arbitration Commission of Bucarest
Decision no. 34, November 29, 1958, *Journal de droit international* (*CLunet*) (1968), p. 426.

First Instance Court of Tehran
Decision December 1, 1963, *National Iranian Oil Company* v. *Sapphire International Petroleums Ltd.*, 9 *International Legal Materials* (1970) 1118.

The Government of the Libyan Arab Republic v. *California Asiatic Oil Company and Texaco Overseas Petroleum Company*, 17 *International Legal Materials* (1978), p. 3.

Libyan American Oil Company (LIAMCO) v. *The Government of the Libyan Arab Republic*, relating to Petroleum Concessions 16, 17 and 20 (*LIAMCO Case*), 20 *International Legal Materials* (1981), p. 1.

British Petroleum Company (Libya) v. *The Government of the Libyan Arab Republic*, (1979) 53 *International Legal Materials*; *Yearbook Commercial Arbitration*, vol V (1980), p. 143.

B.3.2. The state of substantive law on state enterprises and arbitration

European Court of Justice

14.7.1971, Rs. 10/71, *Staatsanwaltschaft Luxemburg* v. *Müller, European Court Reports* XVII (1971), p. 723. Definition of a 'state enterprise' according to Art. 90 EEC.

Conseil d'Etat (Section du Contentieux)

13.12.1957, *Société Nationale de Vente du Surplus*, *Revue de l'Arbitrage* (1958), p. 20.

Cour de Cassation

14.4.1964, *Office National Interprofessionel des Céréales* c. *Capitaine du SS. San Carlo*, *Dalloz* (1964), p. 637, note Robert; *Journal de droit international* (*Clunet*) (1965), p. 646, note Goldman; JCP – *Semaine juridique* (1965) III, 14406, Note P.L.; *Revuse de l'Arbitrage* (1964), p. 82, note Robert p. 137. Public enterprises may submit to arbitration in the presence of an international contract; distinction between *ordre public interne* and *ordre public internationale.*

2.5.1966, *Trésor Public* c. *Galakis*, *Revue de l'Arbitrage* (1966), p. 99; *Journal de droit international* (*Clunet*) (1966), p. 648.

2.5.1978, *Société algérienne de commerce Alco et autres* c. *Sempac et autres*, *Journal de droit international* (*Clunet*) (1978), p. 904, note Ph. Kahn.

Cour d'Appel de Paris

4.5.1976, *Engel* c. *Coopérative agricole de la Mense, Revue del'Arbitrage* (1976), p. 261.

Tribunal de grande instance de Paris

29.11.1972, *Corporacion del Cobre* c. *Société Braden Copper Corporation et Société Le Groupement d'importation des Métaux*,*Journal de droit international* (*Clunet*) (1973), p. 227, note Ph. Kahn. Submission of a state enterprise to arbitration is valuable; no immunity for it acting in international commerce; nationalization.

International Chamber of Commerce, Arbitral Tribunal

Sent. arb. 2521/1975, *Journal de droit international* (*Clunet*) (1976), p. 997. 'Etablissement public'.

Supreme Court of the United States

Alfred Dunhill of London, Inc. v. *Republic of Cuba*, decided May 24, 1976, 16 *International Legal Materials* (1976) p. 735; 425 US 682 (1976); 70 *American Journal of International Law* (1977) 828.

B.3.3. Relevance of being a separate legal entity

Arbitral court attached to the Chamber of Foreign Trade in the GDR

Award SG 257/71, 31.10.1972, in Kammer für Außenhandel der DDR (ed.), *Aus der Spruchpraxis des Schiedsgerichts bei der Kammer für Außenhandel der DDR (1969–1976)*, (East Berlin 1977), p. 57.

Cour de Cassation

February 14, 1978, *Crédit populaire d'Algérie* c. *SAPVIN, Revue critique de droit international privé*, vol. 69 (1980), p. 707, note Mayer.

Hague Court of Appeal

November 28, 1968, *NV Cabolent* v. *National Iranian Oil Company*, 9 *International Legal*

Materials (1970) 152 (English translation); *Nederlandse Jurisprudentie* (1969), No. 484, p. 1329.

President of Rechtbank, Amsterdam
December 14, 1977, *Yearbook Commercial Arbitration*, vol. IV (1979), p. 307.

Court of Arbitration at the Polish Chamber of Foreign Trade in Warsaw
Award February 11, 1958, case no. 17/57, *Yearbook Commercial Arbitration*, vol. VI (1981), p. 147; *Polish Yearbook of International Law*, vol. IX (1977–78) (Warsaw 1980), p. 267.

Court of Appeal (UK)
Krajina v. *The Tass Agency*, [1949] 2 *All England Reports* 274. Even if Tass was a state department having a separate entity, it did not follow that the Soviet government, by procuring its incorporation, had deprived it of the right to assert the immunity normally attaching to a department of a foreign state under international law.
William Cory & Son, Ltd. v. *City of London Corporation*, [1951] 2 *All England Reports* 85.
Baccus SRL v. *Servicio Nacional Del Trigo* [1956] 3 *Weekly Law Reports* 948; [1956] 3 *All England Reports* 715. A separate legal entity which functions as a department of a state is entitled to sovereign immunity; entry of appearance and order for security for costs without knowledge or authority of foreign sovereign and by ignorance of legal rights does not lead to a waiver of sovereign immunity.
Trendtex Trading Corporation Ltd. v. *Central Bank of Nigeria* [1977] 1 *All England Reports* 881. Central bank of foreign state; separate legal entity incorporated by legislative enactment; bank responsible for issue of currency and entrusted with government's banking and foreign exchange transactions too; bank is not a department of state and is not entitled to claim sovereign immunity; incorporation or transaction of international law – theory and practice in England; absolute/restrictive sovereign immunity theory.

Queen's Bench Division (UK)
1° Congreso del Partido [1978] 1 *All England Reports* 1161.

Supreme Court of the United States
Upright v. *Mercury Business Machines Co., Inc.*, *New York Law Journal*, 9.5.1960, p. 12; *Außenwirtschaftsdienst* 1960, p. 157; 55 *American Journal of International Law* (1960) 166. East-German state enterprise; no claim before American courts.
23.3.1964, *Banco Nacional de Cuba* v. *Sabbatino*, 376 US 398; 84 S.Ct. 923. Sovereign Immunity.

United States District Court (North District of Illinois)
Rovin Sales Corp. v. *Socialist Republic of Rumania*, 403 F.Supp. 1298.

United States District Court (District of Columbia)
Edlow International Company v. *Nuklearna Elektrarnna Krsko*, 441 F.Supp. 827.

United States District Court (South District of New York)
Yessesin-Volpin v. *Novosti Press Agency*, 443 F.Supp. 849.

Foreign Trade Arbitration Commission
Award 6.3.1941, *VIO Raznoimport* v. *The Bulgarian Joint-Stock Company Musalla and Trading House Serdika*, in USSR Chamber of Commerce and Industry Law Section (ed.), *Collected Arbitration Cases*, part I, 'Awards of the FTAC 1934–1951' (Moscow 1972), p. 79. Soviet organizations are separate, independent juridical persons; no connection of contracts.

International Chamber of Commerce, Arbitral Tribunal
3093/3100/1979, *Journal de droit international* (*Clunet*) (1981), p. 951, avec observations.

B.3.4. Enforcement of arbitration awards against state enterprises

Schweizerisches Bundesgericht

5.5.1976, *Société des grands travaux de Marseille* c. *Republique populaire du Bangladesh, Bangladesh industrial development corporation, Annuaire du Tribunal Fédéral* 102 Ia, p. 574.

Arbitral Court attached to the Chamber of Foreign Trade of the GDR

Award: SG 284/74, 20.10.1975, in Kammer für Außenhandel der DDR (ed.), *Aus der Spruchpraxis des Schiedsgerichts bei der Kammer für Außenhandel der DDR (1969–1976)*, (East Berlin 1977), p. 51. A sentence for material fulfilment is not enforceable through the arbitration court.

CHAPTER VII

DOCUMENTATION OF MATERIAL RECEIVED

1. INTRODUCTION

As already mentioned in earlier sections of this book, the amount of information and documents received made their reproduction in this book, mainly for financial reasons, impossible, especially since, though by far the greatest part is in English, translations would have been necessary for documents submitted in French, Spanish or German.

Nevertheless, in order to give those especially interested access to the relevant part of the authentic material received, these are made available in photocopied form on demand to readers by using the Order Form on page 115.

The contents of this Documentation of Material Received are reprinted hereafter to give readers an idea of the kind of information available.

2. CONTENTS OF DOCUMENTATION OF MATERIAL RECEIVED

I. *Institute of International Business Law and Practice* (not reproduced, since contained in this book, pp. 1–7, above).

II. *List of contributors to this research* (not reproduced, since contained in this book, pp. 9–10, above).

III. *Introduction, Summary and Conclusions* (not reproduced, since contained in this book, pp. 11–55, above).

IV. *Procedure of the Research* (not reproduced, since contained in this book, pp. 57–63, above).

V. *Proceedings Stockholm Symposium* (either in English or in French without translation).
   A. Programme (not reproduced, see pp. 65–66, above).
   B. List of Participants (not reproduced, see pp. 66–71, above).
   C. Report on Present and Future Activities of the Institute. *Carl-Henrik Winqwist* (12 pages).
   D. Arbitration and State Enterprises: Interim Report. *Karl-Heinz Böckstiegel* (25 pages).

E. Presentations by Panellists
   1. Arbitration and State Enterprises: Case Study of Nigeria Cement Transactions. *Bola Adesumbo Ajibola* (13 pages).
   2. Relevant Practice of the International Chamber of Commerce (in French). *Yves Derains* (6 pages).
   3. Important Aspects of Arbitration and State Enterprises. *William L. Craig*.(16 pages).
   4. Important Aspects of Arbitration and State Enterprises seen from a Third World Country (in French). *Djamal Lakhdari* (13 pages).

F. Discussion (45 pages)
Timm Riedinger
Pieter Sanders
Ole Lando
Bjørn Haug
Reino Erma
Nouz-Eddine Terki
Jean-Paul Retraint
Xavier Tandeau de Marsac
Léon Goffin
Frédéric Eisemann
Jean Robert
Berthold Goldman
Pierre Bellet
Dobrosav Mitrovic

VI. *Synoptical Collection of Answers to Questionnaires* (in English or in French without translation)
- Question 1 (Survey of arbitration practice of state enterprises) (84 pages).
- Question 2 (Survey of practical problems experienced) (51 pages).
- Question 3 (Determination of the applicable law) (58 pages).
- Question 4 (Questionnaire I) (The state of substantive law on state enterprises and arbitration) (31 pages).
- Question 4 (Questionnaire II) (Relevance of varying types of state enterprises for arbitration) (9 pages).
- Question 5 (Relevance of being a separate legal entity) (93 pages).
- Question 6 (Enforcement of arbitration awards against state enterprises) (45 pages).
- Question 7 (Suggestions for improvements) (35 pages).
- Question 8 (Further comments) (10 pages).

VII. *National Reports* (in English, French, German or Spanish without translation)
   1. Argentina (22 pages).
   2. Australia (28 pages).
   3. Austria (22 pages).

4. Belgium (31 pages).
5. Brazil (16 pages).
6. Bulgaria (14 pages).
7. Canada (8 pages).
8. Chile (30 pages).
9. Colombia (23 pages).
10. Czechoslovakia (15 pages).
11. Denmark (3 pages).
12. Finland (22 pages).
13. France (56 pages).
14. Germany, Federal Republic of (49 pages).
15. Germany, German Democratic Republic (14 pages).
16. Great Britain (30 pages).
17. Hong Kong (10 pages).
18. India (14 pages).
19. Indonesia (11 pages).
20. Ireland (12 pages).
21. Italy (40 pages).
22. Korea, Republic of (13 pages).
23. Luxembourg (27 pages).
24. Mexico (10 pages).
25. Morocco (30 pages).
26. Netherlands (5 pages).
27. Nigeria (15 pages).
28. Poland (18 pages).
29. Saudi-Arabia (6 pages).
30. Sweden (17 pages).
31. Switzerland (21 pages).
32. Syria (40 pages).
33. Turkey (23 pages).
34. Uganda (11 pages).
35. United States of America (19 pages).
36. Yugoslavia (12 pages).

VIII. *Reports on Arbitration of Specific International Institutions* (either in English or in French without translation)
   A. International Chamber of Commerce (ICC) (15 pages).
   B. International Centre for Settlement of Investment Disputes (ICSID) (27 pages).
   C. International Air Transport Association (IATA) (20 pages).
   D. North Atlantic Treaty Organization (NATO) (16 pages).

IX. *Bibliography and Collection of Cases*
Not reproduced, but see pp. 73–109, above.

www.ingramcontent.com/pod-product-compliance
Lightning Source LLC
LaVergne TN
LVHW021113300926
849160LV00009B/716
* 9 7 8 9 0 6 5 4 4 1 8 4 3 *